LAY SHEPHERDING

Lay Shepherding

A GUIDE FOR VISITING THE SICK, THE AGED, THE TROUBLED AND THE BEREAVED

RUDOLPH E. GRANTHAM

Judson Press® Valley Forge

Copyright © 1980
Judson Press, Valley Forge, PA 19481
Third Printing, 1981

Unless otherwise indicated, Bible quotations in this volume are from the Revised Standard Ver-
sion of the Bible, copyrighted 1946, 1952, 1971, 1973 by the Division of Christian Education of
the National Council of the Churches of Christ in the United States of America, and are used by
permission.

Library of Congress Cataloging in Publication Data
Grantham, Rudolph E.
    Lay shepherding.

    Bibliography. p.
    1. Church work with the sick.   2. Pastoral
theology.   3. Laity.   I.   Title.
BV4460.G72   253   79-22678
ISBN 0-8170-0863-2

Contents

Introduction

"I myself will be the shepherd of my sheep, and I will make them lie down, says the Lord GOD. I will seek the lost, and I will bring back the strayed, and I will bind up the crippled, and I will strengthen the weak, and the fat and the strong I will watch over; I will feed them in justice" (Ezekiel 34:15-16).

The word of God to Ezekiel is our commission to serve the hospitalized ill or injured, persons in the hospice-caring ministry, the nursing-home resident, the bereaved, persons experiencing family difficulties, the shut-ins, and those in rehabilitation programs. It is a message to those who wish to help their neighbor who is in crisis or whose condition is chronic and who must be sustained if life is to be endured. The commission is for the Christian lay person and the pastor or other persons who will train and/or supervise a lay visitation group.

This book is for those who are beginning a bedside ministry. You, the laity, can and do want to be more involved in the cure of souls. You have the resources and opportunity to leaven all of society with healing, redemptive relationships. This book, as a guide to that ministry, is drawn from experience first as a pastor and then as a chaplain. Most specifically, it is an expression of the value my ministry places on the laity's ministry.

The training topics most helpful in preparing and sustaining laity in ministry are: (1) the authority and context of lay shepherding; (2) the world of those to whom we minister—crisis behavior, grief responses, and the social environment of hospital, nursing home, and the lonely house (the shut-in); and (3) some tools of ministry available to the laity.

This book goes forth with my deep appreciation to my wife Mary, sons Stephen and Mark, and daughter Ruth. Appreciation is also due to my secretary, Mrs. Gene Case, to my doctoral project advisor, Dr. Samuel Southard, and especially to all those laymen and laywomen who shared their experiences so freely and openly. They were my teachers, too.

1

The Authority and Context
for the Lay Shepherding Ministry

**"By what authority are you doing these things . . .?"
(Mark 11:28).**

The first questions a lay visitor asks are ones of humility: "Why was *I* chosen for this work? What authority do I have to visit those in trouble as a representative of the church?"

The answer is in the Scriptures. In the Old Testament, unordained prophets are the lay shepherds. Their concern for people is in a moral context. It is a sin against God to abuse a neighbor (Psalm 51:4). It is a "good" to care for the needy. The classic example is that of Elijah's confrontation of King Ahab over Naboth's vineyard (1 Kings 21). Notice also Nathan's message of judgment to King David (2 Samuel 12:1-13). See also the story of Ruth who, as a poor person, gleaned the fields.

In the New Testament, Jesus is our authority. He trained twelve apostles, none of whom were priests, and a larger group of seventy disciples. And Christian tradition establishes that authority more securely. Deacons were appointed to care for widows (Acts 6). We also note James's instructions to visit, anoint with oil, and pray for the sick.

Today, lay shepherds must meet the same needs, though in different ways. Instead of allowing the gleaning of our fields, we can give food, clothing, or fuel as immediate crisis intervention. And as Christian citizens, we can support job training/retraining programs and sound management of the economy. We can encourage competition and protection from greed-motivated monopolies in our free enterprise economic system.

We should see lay-shepherding opportunities in personal needs as well as a ministry to the social structures.* The Judeo-Christian faiths offer a love-motivated ethic which, if followed, will improve the moral tone of society as well as make it more humane to the individual's needs. But most of all the lay shepherding ministry is the message to a confused and hostile world that God is good, loving, and redemptive. His healing is whole and for ALL his creation.

HEALING FROM A BIBLICAL PERSPECTIVE

1. Certain key words and concepts unlock the biblical meaning of healing. A prominent concept in the Judeo-Christian understanding of healing is "power": "But if it is by the finger of God that I cast out demons, then the kingdom of God has come upon you" (Luke 11:20). The finger of God is a biblical symbol of life-giving power. Michelangelo's *Creation* is a dramatic visual presentation of God's power as He stretches forth His hand to give life to Adam.

"On one of those days, as he was teaching, there were Pharisees and teachers of the law sitting by . . . and the *power* of the Lord was with him to heal" (Luke 5:17, author's italics). Healing is power. It is the power of life over death. It is regenerative power over flesh.

2. The source of healing power is God himself. In the Old Testament, God's love is shown in healing activities. "I am the LORD, your healer" (Exodus 15:26). A shepherd treats his sheep's illnesses as well as providing for their nurture and protection. In Ezekiel 34:15-16, God calls himself such a shepherd. He "binds up the crippled" in addition to his other shepherding functions. The New Testament witnesses that Jesus utilized the power of God to heal (Luke 5:15). Also the followers of Jesus utilized the healing power of God:

"And now, Lord, look upon their threats, and grant to thy servants to speak thy word with all boldness, while thou stretchest out thy hand to heal, and signs and wonders are performed through the name of thy holy servant Jesus" (Acts 4:29-30).

3. The principle characteristics of that healing power are love, compassion, and faith: "As he went ashore he saw a great throng; and he had compassion on them, and healed their sick" (Matthew 14:14; see also Mark 1:40-41; Luke 7:11-15).

---

*This book is not designed to assist one in being a social activist. It is basically pastoral and directed to individual rather than social needs. But recognition of both approaches is acknowledged.

Faith is a power or capacity to make healing power operative. On some occasions it is invoked by Jesus as a prior condition.

> And as Jesus passed on from there, two blind men followed him, crying aloud, "Have mercy on us, Son of David." When he entered the house, the blind men came to him; and Jesus said to them, "Do you believe that I am able to do this?" They said to him, "Yes, Lord." Then he touched their eyes, saying, "According to your faith be it done to you" (Matthew 9:27-29; see also Mark 9:22-24).

Love and faith are present in those who desire healing for a loved one: "And behold, they brought to him a paralytic, lying on his bed; and when Jesus saw their faith he said to the paralytic, 'Take heart, my son; your sins are forgiven'" (Matthew 9:2). But healing also took place where doubt about God's love and power prevailed (see Mark 9:24, "Help my unbelief"); and in the presence of an angry religious establishment, compassion is still operative:

> If a man on the sabbath day receive circumcision, that the law of Moses should not be broken: *are ye angry at me,* because I have made a man every whit whole on the sabbath day? (John 7:23, KJV, author's italics; see also Matthew 12:9-14; Luke 13:10-13; John 5:2-9).

When peace, that is, privacy and quietness, was indicated, Jesus would draw a person aside (Mark 7:31-35).

4. Another key word is *whole.* Christian healing is more than body repair work. People are more than magnificent animals of bone and muscle. We have feelings. We are social creatures, and our relationships are important. But we are also spiritual creatures dependent upon relationships with God. All these dimensions were within the scope of Jesus' healing activity: ". . . I have made a man *every whit whole* . . ." (author's italics; see also Mark 6:56 in KJV).

We see these dimensions of wholeness in Jesus' ministry: He cast out demons (spiritual beings), which may have also been illnesses that have characteristics we assign today to mental illness. He asked a man who had been sick for thirty-eight years if he wanted to get well; hence the will is involved in whole healing. He gave healed people a mission to perform that changed the focus of their lives from self to God's will, his kingdom (Mark 5:19). The family dimension was involved in the use of a parent's (the widow's) faith and the restoring to life of her only son (Luke 7:12). He made use of confession, forgiving a paralyzed man's sin before he gave a healing command and thus showed a moral dimension to whole healing. Spiritual forces were invoked: compassion, faith, and other spiritual powers were at his command and were mediated through his hands and voice in prayer.

5. The moral dimension needs special emphasis. Our secular society and materialistic medicine have not addressed themselves to this relationship. In the Old Testament, healing and forgiveness of sins are treated together (Psalms 103:2-3; 107:17-22; Jeremiah 33:6-9). In the New Testament, James 5:14-16 treats the relationship with a big "IF": "and *if* he has committed sins, he will be forgiven" (author's italics).

How are sins and sickness related? The unredeemed life can be described as a state of sin. But we are justified by the love of God through the acceptance by faith of God's grace through Christ's cross. We enter upon a life of faith in God's kingdom called sanctification. Sins remain, but we are forgiven sinners, growing in grace. It is in this context that we examine behavior called "sins," which may be acts of unlove (sins of commission) or lack of love-motivated activity (sins of omission). It would appear that some sins result in consequences called sickness—for example, gluttony. This is most obvious when toxic chemicals such as alcohol and nicotine are used in excess. One man, ill for thirty-eight years, was told by Jesus: "See, you are well! Sin no more, that nothing worse befall you" (John 5:14).

But Jesus would not let his hearers begin with a sickness and conclude that it was punishment for some sin. When a tower in Siloam fell, Jesus refused to verify the interpretation that those killed were more sinful than others nearby (Luke 13:4). It is interesting that Jesus twice exorcised a demon in a person, and in neither case did he call the sufferer to repentance (Mark 1:21-28; Luke 8:26-39). He did not treat the state of demon possession as a moral problem. In contrast, a victim of paralysis was forgiven first and then given instruction to pick up his bed (Matthew 9:6).

A responsibility dimension is important. A person who overeats, gets fat, has high blood pressure and a stroke is more responsible for such an illness than someone who did not abuse his or her body through irresponsible overeating. Each person is responsible for his or her own sins and no one else's.

"The soul that sins shall die. The son shall not suffer for the iniquity of the father, nor the father suffer for the iniquity of the son; the righteousness of the righteous shall be upon himself, and the wickedness of the wicked shall be upon himself" (Ezekiel 18:20).

One would think that this issue would have been settled years before the Christian era by the prophet Ezekiel, but, no, the idea that God punishes the innocent child for the parent's sin appears in Christian thought today.

6. Healing and salvation are not exactly the same, although they may appear as simultaneous gifts in a person. "Almost a third of the New Testament references to salvation are to restored functions of body, mind, or spirit. . . ."[1] However, the majority of New Testament references to the salvation which Christ brings has to do with deliverance from sin and death.[2]

A brief word study will show the relationship. The Hebrew *shalem* can be translated "healthy" and "whole." It is a cognate of *shalom,* "peace." The Greek word *sozo,* "to save," also means "to make whole from a disease." And the Greek *soter* means "savior" and "healer." Our healing ministry is not merely body repair work. It is restoration to a full (whole) life of harmonious (peace) relationships with Jesus Christ.[3]

Sometimes salvation comes but not healing; Paul had to live with a "thorn in his flesh." The body ages. We cannot expect recovery to return a body to a youthful state of health. Surgery may be only partially successful as in a colon cancer where a colostomy is needed. But a victorious healing attitude would include acceptance of the colostomy and perhaps also volunteer work in helping others accept their surgery. Whole healing strives for as complete physical functioning as possible and, most important of all, a relationship with God that fills the person with spiritual powers greater than any earthly powers or spiritual principalities.

7. The will is important to healing. A man had been ill for thirty-eight years. Jesus asked him, "Do you want to be healed?" (John 5:6). When a person is ill or injured, the will to get well may become medically important. Is the person going home to a loving spouse or to an empty house? Is the person returning to the same dull job, a new job, or no job? Is the illness or accident creating this crisis requiring major life adjustments? If so, does the person have the necessary coping resources? These and other factors make up the healing dimension called "the will to get well."

8. Life-style and values complete our description of Judeo-Christian healing. Affirmation of the good that has happened to us is important. Vows made by temple worshipers were a popular Old Testament response. Gratitude for a blessing reveals character. Ten lepers were healed by Jesus, but only one was grateful and acknowledged God's presence in his healing. We have "death bed conversions." But some people forget their vows upon recovery and engage in the same sinful life-style as before illness.

Compassion (love that suffers with or identifies with another person) motivated Jesus to heal. Compassion also motivates us to share our victory and must be expressed. Sometimes a person is healed and his or her entire life is changed; this person is reoriented toward God, obedient to him, and filled with power and enthusiasm. This was the case with the demoniac (Mark 5:19-20). Jesus refused to let the man become an apostle, telling him instead to witness to his family and neighbors of God's love. In doing this, Jesus did several things. He changed the man's life-style. He removed the self as the center of life and gave him a mission greater than himself, consisting of a meaningful task of helpfulness. When God forgives our sins, he relieves oppressive guilt feelings, and healthy parts of our personality are freed to be used in constructive ways.

HOLISTIC HEALING FROM A CONTEMPORARY PERSPECTIVE

The power of our ministry is the healing presence of Christ. It is he who decides what healing is necessary. A person may pray for physical healing but receive forgiveness and restored relationships as a prelude to physical healing (Matthew 9:2). But not everyone in our society is willing to acknowledge the spiritual dimension in healing. "Wholism" can be the spelling of medicine in a humanistic setting; this involves the body, emotions, and social dimensions. But the spelling should be "holism," for "holy," whenever the spiritual nature of humankind is acknowledged. The two great commandments of Jesus to love God (holism) and to love humankind (humanism) make the spiritual unity of holistic healing. (See Mark 12:28-34.)

The Humanistic Concern

The Body—The initial concern of humanistic medicine is the body. The doctor will address his or her knowledge and skill to physical relief and healing. A small group of nurses and paramedical specialists compose the healing team.

Much scientific research has been conducted into the functioning of the body, its chemistry, and what it takes to restore functions that are not proper. Laboratories study fluid samples from the living body chemistry. Chemists have compounded thousands of drugs for altering body chemistry. Medical science has developed and is still developing surgical skills and physical therapies. It is absolutely fantastic what we can do to and for the body.

The Emotions—But this humanistic approach sees more than flesh and bone. It recognizes an emotional dimension as well. In our recent history we have looked intently and exhaustively at the body.

The amassed knowledge is very impressive, but our prolonged research upon the body has broadened and revealed that people are more than physical chemical factories. Hospitals should be more than body repair shops and doctors more than mechanics and chemists.

All of us know that the emotions affect our bodily state. How often we have been embarrassed because somebody called to the attention of others that we were embarrassed. Quite often we experience a very frightening situation and the sensation of the stomach tightening and indigestion. Also common is the tense situation and the subsequent appearance of a tension headache. One term that some health professionals don't like, but which, I suppose, is the most common term used to designate the relationship between body and emotion, is "psychosomatic." Basically this means that in the production of a particular physical illness there has been a large emotional component of a stressful nature, usually lasting over a long period of time.

In American society, the more commonly encountered psychosomatic disorders are the stomach ulcer, the migraine headache, the backache, and many people are now beginning to conclude that the myocardial infarction form of "heart attack" and angina may be largely the product of stress and emotions. What happens is this. The life stresses and the threats to our well-being, when unrelieved over a long period of time, produce alterations in body chemistry, especially hormone imbalance. This in turn affects the function of an organ. The organs have their own system of interrelationship, and thus the whole person is ill. Scientists have also discovered that stress has a destructive effect upon the body's immune system.

But suppose someone is in the hospital for a cause not brought on by emotional conditions related to the stresses of living. This person may have been an innocent victim in an automobile accident or may have a kidney stone. (So far, I haven't read a theory that we have the power to "psyche up" a kidney stone.) This person might be very angry—angry at the individual who wasn't careful and caused the accident. Or this person may feel guilty because the kidney stone won't pass on its own, and someone is having to do his or her job or is having to take care of home responsibilities. The person may be afraid he or she is going to die, or afraid he or she is going to live (hopelessly) and doesn't really want to live if living means being enslaved to a life-style that is radically restrictive. Patients have deep emotions while physically ill, and we should be *patient* with them.

The Social and Familial Aspects—So far we have said "whole healing" involves a concern for the well-being of the body and emotions if we are to practice a Christian philosophy of healing. But "whole healing" also includes a concern for the patient's relationships with other people. There is no such thing as a solitary illness. Almost everyone has a family. Who then is taking care of the family responsibilities while this young mother is in the hospital? Is the grandmother having to take over? Or an aunt or uncle? Are the older children being pressed into service to take up the slack? What about the person who works outside the home? Who is doing his or her job? Or is it being stacked on the desk or beside the machine awaiting the person's return? When we are ill, people around us are also involved.

Our relationships can "make us or break us." Self-preservation may be the strongest human drive. But we also live *for* others, and when they are no longer *there,* we may also lose our will to get well. Or recovery time may be slowed down, which adds to medical costs. Whole healing *must* address itself to the social dimension. Shepherding has great potential for a compassionate ministry, but it also has a cost-containment contribution.

The Environment—In our own day we have become more aware than ever before that we are dependent upon our environment. No longer can we run roughshod over nature and hope to survive the damage we are inflicting upon it. This concern shows up in the hospital in interesting ways. How often men are seen in the emergency room because they have been damaged by some strong chemical! In the summertime doctors treat a steady stream of sunburn cases—people who have been overexposed to the beneficial rays of the sun. Or perhaps there is an allergy. Occasionally a doctor will tell someone being discharged to air-condition the house and to subscribe to an oxygen service, or a doctor will say that the patient must have a better climate, a drier climate, a higher climate. Yes, we are related to our environment, and we must be aware of its damaging influences as well as of how we can use it constructively. This, too, is part of "whole healing."

Beyond Humanism

We are also spiritual. By this we mean that there is more to life than that which is perceived through the five physical senses. Whole healing is not "whole" until it includes "holism" or "holy." What, then, is included when we say "spiritual"?

The spiritual begins with: (1) the desire to relate to God, universe, unity, cosmic consciousness, etc.; (2) in the Judeo-Christian religions, the meaning of one's life; (3) values (or morality) and life-style; (4) and immortality. All these aspects of reality are usually discussed in a spiritual context.

A Spiritual Relationship with God—The basic need in healing and in prevention of illness is a personal relationship with God. The priority is: first the giver—God—then the gifts. We must relate to God trustingly. He will give us what we need. Dr. Paul Tournier comments upon the value of intimate spiritual communion, whether it be in the Spirit or in a human person:

> It is never as a scientist that the doctor establishes real contact with his patient, but only as a man who feels himself, in spite of his science, as wretched a creature as his patient, sympathizing with him in the true sense of the word: suffering with him.[4]

Suffering *with* us as well as for us is the message of the cross. It is the best answer to "Why does God permit evil, war, suffering, etc.?" We don't really know "why." We do know that he promises to be with us in the experience, and many people have known that promise fulfilled in life-altering ways. Thus do all the threads of life come together, revealing a meaningful pattern, a unity, a oneness.

Healing does not always come through professional "healers." Many authorities come to this conclusion: "Basically, the health-giving force is the spirit of Jesus Christ dwelling in the heart by faith. No limit can be set on the ways in which vital union with Christ quickens the mortal body."[5] And Dr. Tournier says: "It seems that there is a current of physical life which is reestablished on contact with God."[6] R. K. Harrison notes: "It was his [Jesus'] desire that men should be won for the divine kingdom, and share in the powers and energies which were manifested in the relationship existing between him and his Father. . . ."[7]

We do not, cannot, command his presence. We can by faith practice the gifts of the Spirit and rejoice in the fruits evident in our lives. Our shepherding activity can acknowledge the wonder and mystery of his ways to the ill. We can pray that God's will be done. We can trust his love, wisdom, and power to give that which is best for each ill person.

A woman had a hysterectomy, and complications followed. She said: "I was quite ill following my surgery. I saw a light enter the room, and Jesus stood at the foot of my bed. He smiled but did not speak a word. Then he was gone, but I knew at that moment I would be all right."

A woman with a stroke, myocardial infarction, and bilateral pneumonia said to me: "I felt a touch on my forehead. I opened my eyes, but no one was present. I closed my eyes and felt a hand on my forehead. This time I saw a light figure. It was either my sister, who is so close to Jesus, or Jesus himself. I'm not sure. I felt the touch three times." "How did you feel?" I asked. "There was a deep sense of peace, and I felt so relaxed that I went to sleep." I asked if her sister was living. "No, she died ten years ago, but we were very close." The power of spiritual presence produces dramatic religious experiences.

The Meaning of One's Life—The meaning of one's life is not static, not set in concrete. It varies throughout life. During crises it rises to consciousness, and we actively explore the question of meaning. "Why has God left me here?" "What does he want me to do?" Some factors in determining the meaning of one's life are:

1. A personally significant vocation,
2. The love of a family and one's love for the family,
3. Acceptance of and by the community,
4. A sense of destiny, of being loved and used by God,
5. Adequate personal resources for meeting life's problems and opportunities.

All these, taken together, produce a positive, powerful meaning in one's life and become a powerful stimulus to get well. A crisis which takes away one of these factors requires a redefinition of the meaning of one's life. The meaning of one's life is questioned, emotionally if not verbally, by everyone during crises. A "life review" seems to be a part of illness, and the whole healing approach will address itself to this need.

The Moral (Value) Dimension and a Christian Life-style—It is being rediscovered that if we are to heal the body, it is sometimes necessary to handle life's stresses constructively. Much medical treatment is merely symptom relief. Whole healing in a Judeo-Christian context will help the individual discover resources he or she can use to master those life stresses. One resource may be the reordering of one's *values*. This may be necessary before the body can be cured.

Dr. Don Browning, in commenting upon Dr. Karl Menninger's book *Whatever Happened to Sin?*, stresses the moral and value confusion in today's world. Value confusion contributes to emotional problems, sickness, and identity confusion. He states: "One of the strongest assets to good mental health is the existence of a relatively firm and accurate moral universe which gives indices to the good and suggests appropriate actions to reach the good."[8] Dr. Browning stresses to a role-confused church that religion has traditionally offered a culture the highest "controlling values and value symbols."[9] He finds in our Judeo-Christian tradition the foundation for a morally relevant church and would combine the Old Testament covenant law in the form of "practical moral rationality"[10] with the early church's hope and experience of the kingdom of God as a present, partially acquired reality to be consummated in the future.[11] He calls upon the church to be a "center for moral discourse and decision making."[12] A church functions best when its care takes place in this moral context.

An interesting confirmation of the moral dimension's application to health care comes from Dr. Victor E. Fuchs, a medical economist. In *Who Shall Live?* the author considers the importance of one's "life-style" and personal behavior on "who shall live."

> The greatest current potential for improving the health of the American people is to be found in what they do and don't do to and for themselves. Individual decisions about diet, exercise, and smoking are of critical importance, and collective decisions affecting pollution and other aspects of the environment are also relevant. . . . As René Dubos has acutely observed, "To ward off disease or recover health, men as a rule find it easier to depend on the healers than to attempt the more difficult task of living wisely."[13]

The moral dimension, after a time of neglect and denial, is reentering the American character and consciousness. Our life-style is killing many of us, as well as those around us. The summation of faith in God is a sacrificial life-style motivated by love. We have received abundantly; we will want to give abundantly.

Immortality—"He was not living." "She was not the person we all know." "He is not suffering now." Statements such as these affirm that life is more than a complicated chemical factory and a fantastic computer called a "brain." Some people spin philosophical arguments for and against immortality in philosophy's academic armchair. But the bedside chair in the hospital room produces a different kind of thinking. Our hearts desperately yearn for the certainty of life after this life in the flesh.

The Bible gives us the assurances we need in the face of death: "'He will wipe away every tear from their eyes, and death shall be no more, neither shall there be mourning nor crying nor pain any more, for the former things have passed away'" (Revelation 21:4). Humanism is good, but is it good enough? Who can do without the presence of God in this life as a present resource and assurance of future fulfillment! When physical healing cannot be our goal, life eternal should be.

Whether we begin with the Master Physician Jesus Christ and the witness of the Bible or with the demands of delivering quality health care today, we arrive at the same place. Healing activities must be directed to the whole person. And when healing does not come, comfort must be given to patient and family.

It may seem that this chapter's major stress has been placed on physical healing. The illustrations drawn from my experience can account for this. Thus, a balancing statement should be made. Physical healing may not come from the medical doctor whose treatment can be only symptomatic relief. Healing may come only when, for instance, one's marriage is no longer sick. Or, vice versa, a healthy marriage may be a deterrent to physical illness. The lay shepherd and the church may be quite valuable here. One's life-style may be the stress which causes a person's periodic mental breakdown. On the other hand, a Christian life-style which is in harmony with God's spiritual laws will direct a person's life-style so that it harmonizes with physical laws. Thus, physical and mental health is the fruit. Christian community may be more sustaining than periodic visits to a mental specialist. (These two therapies, however, should not be placed in opposition to one another.) Inadequate secular coping devices may need to be supplemented with prayer and Bible study groups, since the latter two are means for tapping God's guidance, love, and power. Thus, God himself will provide prevention of illness and wholeness in all areas of life: personal, family, and social.

It just may be that the recovery of lay shepherding and Christian community will prove the most effective and least costly (financially) therapy for American society.

THE CONTEXT OF LAY SHEPHERDING

How do we participate today in the spirit of Christ's healing ministry?

Like the church's apostles, we, too, go about preaching, teaching, and healing. We use the same gifts of the Holy Spirit as they are listed by Paul: utterance of wisdom, utterance of knowledge, faith, healing, working of miracles, prophecy, ability to distinguish between spirits, tongues, interpretation of tongues (see 1 Corinthians 12:4-11). In all of church history we see the healing/shepherding activities. If they are not part of the mainstream theological or programming activities, they can be found in the monastic orders or at shrines, or in sects or fringe church groups which have elevated healing to a high priority.

Following this apostolic example, the history of the Christian church has often seen the mobilizing of nonordained Christians of "good repute, full of the Spirit and of wisdom" (Acts 6:3). Two examples illustrate this lay shepherding ministry. Dr. John McNeill writes:

> Side by side with the parish ministry of the priestly confessor there has flourished in Russia the work of guidance of a class of devout and spiritually experienced men known as elders *(starets,* plural: *startsy)* many of whom are not in priestly orders, yet exercise an authoritative direction of souls.[14]

He adds that in Dostoevski's *The Brothers Karamazov,* Zossima is such an elder.

Lay shepherding expressed through the principles of mutual edification and fraternal correction, consolation and discipline, nurture and rebuke for sins, was also prominent in eighteenth- and nineteenth-century Protestantism. John Wesley, the founder of Methodism, came to Georgia to convert the Indians. But he found his "main design" a closed door. He wrote in his second Savannah *Journal:*

> . . . we considered in what manner we might be most useful to the little flock in Savannah. And we agreed (1) to advise the more serious among them to form themselves into a sort of little society, and to meet once or twice a week, in order to reprove, instruct, and exhort one another, (2) To select out of these a smaller number for a more intimate union with each other, which might be forwarded, partly by our conversing singly with each, and partly by inviting them all together to our house; and this, accordingly, we determined to do every Sunday. . . .[15]

We see a resurgence of interest in shepherding and healing today, but we must look at the recent enthusiasm with caution. How can we minister in a manner that is consistent with our spiritual mission and cooperative with other medical efforts? The following chapters are concerned with this question.

2

The Christian's Ministry to Those in Crisis

The shepherding ministry often begins when there is a crisis. In the first emotional reaction, crisis is seen in purely negative terms—as a threat. But the threat may also contain possibility for growth and good. Thus we will work with this definition: *A crisis is a situation or event in someone's life which is perceived as threatening to a vital need and possibly catastrophic, but also harboring the potential for growth.* *

CRISIS THEORY

A crisis is perceived as a threat to a person's needs (job, health, spouse's love, sanity, etc.). Some typical crises in those hospitalized are illness, accident, and death of a loved one. Moving to a nursing home is a major crisis. Domestic problems such as runaway children, teenage crime, divorce, unemployment, etc., are also crises which invite lay-shepherding ministry. The subject will be discussed under three headings: personal, family, social.

Personal

A crisis often has a vortex or whirlpool effect, drawing into its destructive whirl other problems and consequences as the initial crisis develops. Loss of one's business, job, or possessions may be followed by periods of emotional stress, grief, floundering, excessive drinking

*The following description of crisis is heavily indebted to the research of Dr. Gerald Caplan[1] and is supplemented by my experience in pastoral work as a local church minister and hospital chaplain.

of alcohol, mental disorder, and possibly treatment and hospitalization. Illness, especially when it leads to hospitalization, is a crisis in which one's life-style may be threatened; it may cause an experience such as an early retirement, or life itself may be threatened. At best, one's personal schedule is disrupted, and possibly there will be disruption of family roles. The person hospitalized may respond with anguish or quiet satisfaction (glad to get a rest or to escape for a short time from an overwhelming problem).

As a crisis develops, the person applies his or her long-used, habitual, problem-solving techniques ("re-equilibrating mechanisms"). However, they do not work in the same time frame as before, and other problem-solving methods are tried. Meanwhile strong and threatening emotions of a stress and grief nature, such as anger, guilt, hopelessness, anxiety, and fear build and complicate the mental activity directed at solving the crisis. Thus these emotions also become part of the problem as the whirlpool effect continues. But there may also be a buildup of positive emotions and a strengthening of one's will to fight. One wife said, "My husband's cancer was slow. It gave me time to prepare. Now I think I am as ready as anyone can be."

But when traditional problem-solving methods do not work, the person may experiment with solutions new to him or her. Some even "try religion." The nominal church member may pray or go to church services, hoping to get some help. In a crisis the person is much more open to suggestions from others who seek to be helpful.[2]

If the illness is disfiguring, as with burns, or it results in permanent loss because of amputation or stroke, the result can be permanent alterations in the style of life as well as a radical change in self-image. This change in self-image will add to the crisis, and the person and his or her family must deal with it emotionally as it affects the family members' own relationships and social relationships. Especially hard to understand is the mentally altered, frequently hostile patient.

Finances may be an added problem. Not only may the family watch the hospital bill increase above the major medical insurance coverage, but there are also immediate out-of-pocket expenses: transportation, food, and possibly housing (motel) and baby-sitting expenses. In addition, one or both spouses may experience loss of salary.

A more serious problem is the inability to return to one's former job. Retraining may be necessary, and often financial assistance during the retraining period is required. The stress on a family during this time can be considerable, and the church's supportive ministry is valuable.

The patient may see the family exhausted, fearful, and sick. Their distress becomes an added worry. If the members of the family are eating properly, getting adequate rest, and are filled with the spiritual gifts of faith, hope, and love, then they influence the patient positively. But if the family is subconsciously identifying with the patient's pain by not eating or getting adequate rest and if they are filled with anxiety and fear, then the patient has another worry: the effects of his or her illness on the family. In this case the patient's physical condition may not be helped but instead is hindered.

A person's perception of the crisis is important. Some people crumble under the least problem. Others bear loads which demand the onlooker's admiration. Why the difference? Some people have developed good problem-solving techniques, have good support communities, and have developed personal character during previous crises which strengthens them in the present. We will look at this factor later in the chapter. We also see people who respond to crisis with denial as one extreme and overdependency upon others as another extreme reaction.

Family

A hospital volunteer saw the chaplain coming up the stairs and waited for him. "Chaplain, I've just taken a new patient to his room. *He* is fine, but his wife is crying profusely! Think you can help her?"

"Chaplain, are we glad to see you!" Chaplains learn to recognize panic messages in the voices of coronary care unit nurses: "We have two families out there" (pointing to the waiting room) "who are driving *us* crazy and are doing harm to the patients."

The crisis of hospitalization is a family crisis, and it is a well-known fact that families can help or hinder the patient's recovery. The total effect of crisis is a maze of interpersonal dynamics, personality variables in patients and family members, and external factors, especially the efforts of professional and informal helpers. In many cases, the lay visitor's first contacts are with the family rather than the patient. Sometimes the visitor will never see the patient, especially in intensive and coronary care units. Let us look at this complex interaction.

Initially the family may experience a surge of strength, supported by hope and faith in God, in themselves, in medical science, and in the other professional helpers who give reassurance and support. But as the crisis continues, there will inevitably be a steady erosion of physical, emotional, and spiritual strength as fatigue takes its toll. Often the family's strength can be seen to wax and wane; ". . . when the strain mounts too high, fatigue produces a blunting of perception and a resting or recuperative phase."[3] Sometimes a family member collapses from fatigue or becomes sick; the strain might also be manifested in an alcoholic binge or a drug trip.

Family members may experience many of the same personal dynamics seen in the person experiencing a crisis. We have said that a crisis is a threat to a need. The family is threatened with the loss of a valued member, and thus the crisis of one member creates personal crisis reactions in the others.

But a crisis also creates problems at the family level of interaction. Personal and social responses are of necessity interrelated. The "well" spouse (assuming there is no crisis here, but sometimes multiple illnesses exist) finds sexual and emotional needs unmet. The mother/wife may be especially torn, wanting to give support to the husband and also seeing the children's needs unmet. The dependent children are doubly hit. Not only have they lost the support of the parent in crisis, but they have also lost the support of the well parent who is away with the ill spouse and who is also emotionally exhausted. Often, we see the larger family—grandparents, aunts, and uncles—come in to help at this point.

Traditional family roles and the decisions made by members in those roles may be upset. For example, the sick husband may be unable to write checks, and the wife is "lost" in a complicated billing maze. Or, to his chagrin, some of his roles as family provider and leader may be assumed by another family member who later does not want to relinquish that new role. Schedules of well family members, such as car pool assignments, appointments, etc., are upset, and these frustrations are added to an already tense emotional situation. These extra duties may be placed upon neighbors or children or extended family, such as grandparents.

The family's internal relationship structure can help or hinder the crisis-resolution efforts. The interpersonal roles of the members may be confused and chaotic. The family itself may use poor problem-solving methods which it forces upon the patient. These may be in conflict with the efforts of professional helpers. An example would be when cirrhosis of the liver or pancreatitis caused by alcoholism is covered up by denial that the person's drinking is greater than the "social" level.

Social

In some situations the community may be threatened, as in the case of a crime, infectious disease, or a major weather-related disaster such as a flood or tornado. In these social crises emotional reactions can include mass panic and/or withdrawal as well as the individual reactions commonly seen in crises. But the community also has healing and sustaining individuals. Beyond the family are helpers, informal and professional. Dr. Caplan states that distress in someone triggers in others a desire to help. This response "appears to have primitive biosocial roots; similar phenomena can be found in many social animals."[4]

Lay shepherds can be placed in the category of informal helpers. Some informal helpers are naturally endowed with helping attitudes and the ability to give sound advice. They are sought out if they are known by reputation. Others, "busybodies," because of personal neuroses, thrust themselves and their faulty problem-solving methods upon the patient. Too often one hears: "If you will repent, God will heal you." "You are being punished by God for your sins." Sometimes magical intervention by God is promised: "If you have enough faith, God will heal you." Seldom, if ever, does the helper assume responsibility for giving bad advice if "faith" fails. And if the promised relief does not come, the poor patient feels even more guilty for not having had enough faith.

ASSESSING A CRISIS FOR HELPFUL INTERVENTIONS

It is impossible to list all the specific acts of helpfulness that would be appropriate to all cases of need. But a *helping strategy is essential and must begin with an assessment of the nature of this particular crisis.* Here are some variables to be considered by helpers who wish to assist a person or family in crisis.

1. What are the person's habitual (previously used) problem-solving techniques? (See Dr. Howard Clinebell's problem-solving methods which follow.)

2. How threatening does the person believe the problem to be? What may be perceived as a person-destroying crisis to one person may be an "ordinary" problem for another.

3. What were the person's prior health and mental attitude? How are they now? For example, is this the third heart attack or surgery in the past six months? Is the patient depressed now but

was not before, or very weak physically now in contrast to the first hospitalization?

4. Does the personality of the person—character and values— reflect available strength to be mobilized?

5. Was the crisis a result of chance or fate (in the wrong place at the wrong time), or did the patient bring the crisis upon himself or herself by some action?

6. What is the quality of communication between the person and his or her family or the person and the community's helping agencies?

7. Does the family possess resources that can be used? If so, what are they? Resources would include those appropriate to the crisis-resolving activity.

8. What is the availability of community sources for help? For example, some rural communities have no mental health facilities in the community.

A HELPING STRATEGY

A helping strategy based on your assessment of a crisis should have several characteristics. The assessment strategy above and this helping strategy were developed in my lay-training sessions. Imaginative planning "on paper" can help prepare the visitor for a better visit.

1. Focus upon the problems and needs in the particular crisis. You may be able to supply the deficiency or see that it is met. Remember, a crisis is a threat to an important need in someone's life.

2. Use the strengths of that person, his or her family, and the community, especially the religious community. Dr. Caplan lists the strengths of a group helpful to a person in crisis. They are: mutual acceptance of the various members' role and authority, and open, honest communication.[5] These same strengths can be mobilized to help the family members who are experiencing aspects of the loved one's crisis.

3. Your strategy should encourage the patient and family to assume personal decision making and responsibility. If they fall into the trap of overdependency upon you, consult with the pastor or someone else who can assist you out of this situation. It does good neither to you nor to the person being helped for a chronic dependency relationship to continue.

4. Go slow in the giving of advice. No one possesses all the information needed to make a decision for another. If advice is offered, ask the person to evaluate it and make his or her own decision.

5. If you feel that you are "over your head" or that the person needs the services of some specialist, be prepared to discuss this with the pastor if your program is under his or her direction. If not, then suggest referral for help for this particular need. Referral is not always letting a person go completely beyond your care and concern. A supportive ministry can be maintained while special needs are being met by a specialist. Indeed, sometimes supportive care is necessary so that one is able to marshal the necessary strength to contact and follow through a referral treatment.

6. Whole healing is our goal. Where healing is only partial, sustaining ministry takes over. Therefore, the church as a moral community concerned with the total person should promote personal religious growth and the search for a meaningful future life-style through its crisis and support ministry.

CONSTRUCTIVE WAYS OF DEALING WITH CRISES

Dr. Howard Clinebell has listed several constructive ways for coping with crises.[6] In using these coping behaviors and attitudes, the person may experience character growth, and his or her problem-solving efforts will be positively reinforced.

These crisis-coping devices include *facing the problem*. We must admit to ourselves that a problem exists before we can begin working on it. Denial is a common reaction to threat.

Next, we should *enlarge our understanding of it*. What factors make up the crisis? One is emotions, which may be either stimulating or paralyzing. Another is one's attitude toward the problem. This would include one's faith response. Other factors are social: finances, vocation, actions by other persons, etc. If the crisis is physical, how much damage has the body sustained? What is the recovery possibility?

A person must *express and "work through" negative feelings* such as resentment, anxiety, or fear. This can most easily be done with other persons and with God in prayer.

The person must *accept responsibility for coping with his or her own problem*. Each of us must make his or her own decisions.

Crises can often be resolved by more than one solution; so *explore alternative strategies and solutions* by evaluating possible reactions of others and the consequences of each possible solution.

Separate the changeable from the unchangeable elements in the crisis. The "Serenity Prayer" (also called the "AA Prayer") reads, "God, grant me the serenity to accept the things I cannot change, courage to change the things I can, and wisdom to know the difference." With this wisdom, we must accept the unchangeable: a heart muscle has been damaged, a limb is gone, a disease is not reversible, the house has burned, a spouse is dead.

Surrender grandiose and burdensome aspects of one's self-image. That is, accept those parts of your personality and behavior that trouble you and of which you are not proud.

Open channels of communication with others who can help. We are not expected to be self-sufficient. As someone has said, "Even the Lone Ranger has Tonto."

Finally, *decisions must be put into action.* It does little good merely to talk and think. We must "act to alter" the situation.

THE POWER IN THE LAY SHEPHERD'S CRISIS MINISTRY

Dr. Caplan suggests that the people who have the most influence on someone in a crisis are "those who are linked to him by the primary bonds of his basic needs for love and interaction and those who fit in with his needs for authority and dependence."[7] The power of authority and dependence in our everyday relationships is astounding. Its influence in crisis can be more healing than anything else done for a person. What is your relationship to the person being visited in terms of authority? What is the level of the person's dependence upon you?

A patient was in the cardiac unit and had developed a severe depression. Neither the pastor nor I (the hospital chaplain) could help him. One day his boss secured permission to visit the patient in the cardiac unit. He said, "George, I want you to know that effective the first of this month I've given you a $1,000 a year raise and hired a young assistant to do the heavy part of your job." The patient's depression lifted immediately!

A son-in-law who had a very close relationship with his father-in-law was told that the man had given up and that there was no physical reason for the depression. The son-in-law stood by the bed and said, "Pop, if you want to die, die. That's your privilege. But you aren't going to die this way. You have always smiled and had a good time. Now smile. Right now! Die smiling!" The old man opened his eyes, smiled, and two weeks later went home to live another year before a different illness took him.

The power of a wife's love *and* fear motivated a man to live:

Everyone needs someone to love him deeply. During my hospitalization, I was quite ill. Fear that I would die was very strong at first. It was in this time that I reached out to my wife for strength. As her arms encircled me, I felt strengthened. At the same time, I felt her fear. Just as I needed her, so did she need me. My fear of death left. A strong resolve to live and to get well replaced it. A grim determination to fight off death became a conscious concern.

I thanked God for my doctor and for the hospital staff. They worked hard, but so had I! Because of their love and my wife's love, I'm going home.[8]

Whether a boss or spouse, friend or in-law, we all should determine the value and use of authority and dependence in our helping relationships.

BEYOND THE BEST IN HUMANISTIC CRISIS RESOLUTION

We often think we know what is best for someone. But do we? The assessment inventory of a crisis is not infallible. People often withhold information. Diagnostic equipment and tests have their limits. And the person is dynamic, not static, and thus is constantly changing, responding to and changing his or her environment and person. The best in humanistic concern, diagnosis, and treatment should be used, BUT the lay shepherd also has prayer. Seek God's guidance and trust him to do that which is most appropriate. Instead of petitioning God to give what appears to you to be an answer to a need, ask instead that God's wholeness might fill a person. More will be said on this in the chapter on prayer, but here it needs to be emphasized that faith in the wisdom, love, and power of God are essential to successful crisis resolution.

CHRISTIAN EQUIVALENTS OF CRISIS RESOLVING ACTIVITIES

We are greatly indebted to students of human behavior, such as Dr. Caplan, for mapping the contours of crisis behavior. But the Christian faith has powerful and unique resources for support in and resolution of crises.

I asked a question of six friends of admirable faith and life. In answering, several related a personal crisis previously unknown to me. They shared how, in their crisis, God had sustained them through their faith. The question I asked was: *When your life has been its roughest and you were severely tested or tempted, how did you handle it?* It was a spiritual revelation as the following pattern emerged.

After a time of deepening crisis, prayer took on an intensity of expression not present before. Prayer was persistent, intense, and offered many times during the day. When instruction or answers to their prayers were received, these persons felt a deep commitment to "do it"!

What did they say to God in prayer? "I told him exactly what was on my mind and exactly how I felt." They admitted to God that they did not know what to do and felt that they could do nothing. Weak faith and confession were included. Like the father of a boy healed by Jesus, they prayed, "Lord, I believe; help my unbelief." And they confessed, "Forgive me of my wrongs in this matter."

Then they asked God for strength to do what had to be done, for patience to last out the storm, and for moral guidance to improve their lives. One person said, "Jesus set the pattern of prayer for us by his prayers. God answered his, and he will answer our prayers when we pray as Jesus did." Usually after describing how they prayed and the content of their prayers, my friends commented upon their understanding of God. They were not alone; someone was with them in the crisis; there was a Presence! They were bathed in love, and they knew it was God's love.

God was experienced as strength. What they could not do, God could do for them. They felt they could trust him to do what was right. So they prayed, "Thy will be done." With this affirmation, they left the crisis in his hands and waited patiently for the outcome. When the answer came, they *knew* it was the awaited answer. It was often delayed (according to their expectations, for they wanted relief), and it came when least expected. But an answer was given.

The second activity in crisis resolution was a request to others for prayer. And these people *did* pray. Their friends called and visited and told them of prayer groups and other individuals who were praying. They believed that sometimes a person could be so overwhelmed by a problem that he or she could not "get through." But God would hear the prayers of "a righteous man" (James 5:16) and woman! These friends were sustained by their own friends and families and their larger family—the church. The request for prayer by others actually resulted in the mobilization of community support.

Two of my friends added a third comment: They studied their Bibles more carefully. In their deep distress they searched for comforting passages that reassured them of God's love and wisdom and benevolent power. Thus they tapped the strength of their Christian heritage, which has a characteristic making this possible: Vicarious participation in the biblical experiences can be verified in our own spiritual life. My friends' experience with Scripture explains the popularity of the Psalms; we, too, have followed in the psalmists' experiences of despair and victory. The Christian's response to crisis is intimate communion with God through prayer and Scripture and the special supportive help and prayer of family, friends, and the Christian community.

If the activities of these six persons are carefully analyzed, they are found to correspond to the behavior which both Dr. Caplan and Dr. Clinebell describe as conducive to mental health. The six friends accepted the fact that they each had a problem. In prayer they analyzed the problem and sought solutions. Emergency measures in the form of more intense and frequent prayer were employed. They reached beyond their own resources to God's help and to the help of friends. Their community of faith supported them with its resources. My friends worked through their guilt in prayer, "surrendering grandiose and burdensome aspects" of the self, and accepted their limited abilities. They trusted and waited for the love, wisdom, and benevolent power of God to intervene redemptively. When the answer came through prayer, they acted upon the answer, thereby taking constructive action.

Crisis resolution for the Christian is directed toward "wholeness" and "holiness." For not only did these friends' lives give witness to their sound mental health, but they were also vibrant witnesses to the love of God and were his servants to others in need.

In the above cases, the object of the need being threatened by crisis was restored; at times the object is permanently lost. Dr. Caplan advises that the person should be helped to grieve and relinquish the loss and find suitable substitutes. Happily for this situation, the church is in a position to help. It offers a supportive ministry. This ministry will be discussed in chapter 9.

Crisis ministry sees problems in the context of a life beyond this life in the flesh. "He [God] will wipe away every tear from their eyes, and death shall be no more, neither shall there be mourning nor crying nor pain any more, for the former things have passed away" (Revelation 21:4). Many people express this reality by such faith phrases as "He is better off now; he is out of pain." "Mom was not living; she was existing. She's with Dad now." "She was prepared to go as well as anybody could be."

Christians can bear the brokenness of this life because of God's present strength. But when that brokenness cannot be mended, they are strengthened by a hope that testifies to a life which is complete.

3
Ministering to Those Who Grieve

Grief is one of the most commonly experienced human conditions. It is a reaction to loss. Job said that death is the way of all flesh. We could add that it is also a hard way. Great is the agony we experience when the love for the lost one is great! Sometimes the depth of our grief is the measure of our love.

Grief is a complex experience with emotional, physical, social, and spiritual components. It may include anger, guilt, regressions, meaninglessness in regard to one's life, depression, and hopelessness. Physical pains of unknown origin and even illness of a stress nature may appear after a short time of bereavement. Grief may even be prior to the loss. In this case it is called anticipatory grief. This prior response to loss can oftentimes cushion the loss when it does occur.

Though we recognize that grief may be for any object, image, or concept that has been lost, the emphasis in this treatment of grief will be upon loss by death of significant persons. An additional emphasis in this chapter will be on the grief seen in accident and illness. But a treatment of grief cannot be limited to this setting since a thorough understanding of the total experience is necessary for an adequate ministry to those grieving.

The following are some situations in which we grieve:

1. Loss of a loved person;
2. Loss of parts of the body, internal (womb, lung, etc.) and external (foot, finger, etc.), or bodily functions (sexual, mental, etc.);

3. Loss of our concept of ourselves;
4. Moving to a new town or across town;
5. Broken engagement, "Dear John" letter, or divorce.

THE MOURNING PROCESS

The mourning process varies from individual to individual and manifests itself differently in the several stages of life. We may have consciously forgotten a childhood grief experience simply because it was not a very emotional experience. But one's adult values and perhaps even one's vocational selections may be, in part, a result of that experience. Senior citizens may feel the results of mourning in an increase in health problems. Our plan is to examine the grief process by stages in life, beginning with childhood. We will then look at helping adults grieve, then at helping children grieve.

Children

Children and youth tend to show their grief through behavior. These include: (1) playing "dead," perhaps playing the undertaker or minister following the funeral; (2) aggression and anger shown in breaking toys or hurting other children; (3) abandonment fantasies— being left alone is terrifying; (4) substitution of other feelings for true ones—for example, being boisterous in an effort to overcome the blues. Dominant feelings seen in children are fear, uncertainty, insecurity, and sadness. The antidote for them is love, information, patience, understanding, playing games, and the reassurance that you will not leave the child.

Dr. Edgar Jackson notes that children's reactions seem to be cumulative, beginning with a sense of loss (ages birth to four), biological concerns (four to seven), social and relationship concerns (eight through twelve), and psychological and philosophical/religious concerns (teen years). In the adult grief experience, all these elements are present since the grief experience is cumulative.[1]

Young and Middle-Aged Adults

Young adults and middle-aged people tend to show their grief chiefly through emotional outlets and relationship behavior. The first major work in adult grief was done by E. Lindemann working largely with the survivors of the Coconut Grove Nightclub fire. Lindemann observed five dominant initial responses to loss: (1) somatic distress, (2) preoccupation with the image of the deceased, (3) guilt, (4) hostility, (5) loss of patterns of conduct.[2]

There is an initial shock upon learning of a close loved one's death, characterized most often by denial and/or unbelief, accompanied by somatic and emotional disturbances. There are also some long-term reactions to loss. Guilt centers around unresolved conflict and thoughts of love unexpressed or things done. Anger may be experienced toward the loved one, but it is taboo to criticize the dead; often this anger is directed toward the doctor, the hospital, God, the church, or any other convenient figures. Depression, loneliness, and withdrawal from normal activities are to be expected. The pain of being alone in a couples' world, of going alone to familiar happy places must be dealt with gently and patiently by the person and by those who would help. Sanity may be questioned. This *is* a stressful time, and dreams, nightmares, and preoccupation with the image of the deceased are often strange new experiences.

The heavy stresses of adjustment include learning to do the business formerly done by the deceased, settling the estate, possibly dealing with crank telephone calls and con artists seeking to make an illegal "sale." The widow or widower may be father *and* mother and may be trying to help children with their grief. Illnesses of a stress nature often appear, especially "nerves" and gastric disorders.

After several months, hope begins to be experienced. The waves of sorrow are not so large and are further apart. First anniversary dates are difficult: birthdays, Christmas, wedding anniversary, first anniversary of death. Finally, the mourner adjusts to the loss. Life's energies are reinvested in the lives of others, other service causes, and sometimes vocations. Some pain always remains, but it is manageable.

Older Adults

Following Edgar Jackson's conclusion that grief is a cumulative experience that includes all prior responses in our maturation, we may add the observation that older adults will show their grief through physical symptoms. This should not be surprising since the body is usually much weaker from "wear and tear" than it was in youth. Probably the weakest parts of the body first show the stress and strains. "Hypochondriasis" is the word doctors use to designate physical pains associated with anxiety:

The hypochondriacal person will express considerable anxiety and tension around a physical concern rather than the loss and its consequences. Examination usually establishes no demonstrable basis for the presenting complaint. The bereaved person who becomes hypochondriacal may interpret symptoms of a tension headache as representative of a brain tumor and become agitated over that belief. Arthritic shoulder pain is often interpreted as heart disease; constipation and loss of appetite— common symptoms of grief and/or depression—become indicators of malignancy. Rather than reacting to a symptom in terms of its most probable cause, a remote possibility is given total credence.[3]

One study showed that "bereaved relatives were found to have a much higher mortality rate during the first year of bereavement" (12.2% compared to 1.2% in the control group).[4]

It is important to understand that these persons are expressing their strong anxiety, anger, fear and guilt feelings through these physical symptoms.[5]

Some questions raised by these studies are: Would more active counseling and support result in grief being expressed in other, less-harmful ways? Should the church organize itself to meet these grief needs in a more-effective manner? Should our concept of prevention of illness be expanded to cover grief work as a prevention of so many stress illnesses seen after a great loss?

SYMPTOMS OF PATHOLOGICAL GRIEF

Grief can become an occasion for other, more-serious behavior to emerge in the life of the person:

1. Continuing withdrawal from normal activities and relationships;
2. The absence of grieving by acting as though nothing important has happened (denial);
3. Severe prolonged depression with suicidal thoughts and actions;
4. Inability to orient oneself in space and time;
5. Marked personality changes—sometimes the survivor will act out parts of the personality of the deceased;
6. Severe, prolonged guilt and/or anger;
7. Escape via alcohol, other drugs, and religious activity.

HELPING A PERSON MOURN

The title of this section is accurately stated. Those who counsel us not to mourn are false counselors. We must mourn. Paul in 1 Thessalonians 4:13 says we are not "to grieve as others do who have no hope." He never says not to mourn but encourages faith in God which permits us to hope in eternal life, which becomes a blessing in our grief. "Throughout the grief counseling process the guiding principle is this: *The experiencing and working through of painful feelings is an indispensible part of the healing!* Blocked feelings = delayed or blocked healing."[6]

Our goals as helpers should be tailored to each person, but general goals for all can be: (1) to accept the person, (2) to facilitate the "working through" of feelings, and (3) to help the person find new meaning in life.

The Latin root for religion, *religio,* is "to bind together" or "to center." This is a helpful concept to apply when using religious faith and resources to help persons in mourning.

Helping Adults Mourn

There are many responses which the lay shepherd can give to those who need help "working through" their grief. Many of the following suggestions are applications of the principles of redemptive listening found in chapter 6.

1. Encourage the person to express freely his true feelings, especially the negative ones of anger, guilt, unworthiness, etc. Talking is an especially helpful emotional release. Don't argue about guilt being unjustified. It may or may not be, but the point is that the grieving person sees it as justified. Angry words are safer when expressed in the presence of the helping person. If they are not and are "unloaded" on someone else, they may do much damage and have to be "eaten" later.

2. Don't try to divert the person from talking about the loss and related problems. The weather is not more important. Grief brings radical life-style alterations which must be worked through. Respond to the person, not to the anxiety raised in you by the topic of death, anger, or guilt, etc.

3. Don't be afraid to talk about the person who has died. Help by recalling pleasant associations and memories. Days or weeks later, you might ask: "How are things? I've come by to see if I can be of help." Help at this point is often very crucial.

4. Don't be afraid of causing tears or emotional pain. Your friendship will cushion the pain and make it less difficult than if the person had to bear it alone. Besides, you never know what comment will bring tears, and to be fearful of causing them is to stifle conversation.

5. Let the person draw strength from you. There is healing in your warmth and love and in your gift of time to listen.

6. If you are a close friend, consider visiting often the first two months. But whether or not there is a close friendship, a person should not be left alone for too long a time. Search for reasons to do things together. Fishing, grocery shopping, buying the auto tag,

turning in taxes, etc., are helpful activities, not only for their friendship value. The widow(er) may be doing this activity for the first time and could be anxious about how it is done.

7. Encourage the person to discover how much he or she has left in life. Encourage him or her to tell what life holds. If this topic provokes anger, consider confronting the person with this reaction and asking what it means. Remember that timing is important in the selection of some counseling topics.

8. Encourage the person to keep active. Free tickets to bazaars and ball games or invitations to attend activities with you can accomplish this.

9. Help the person begin doing things for others. Service is the antidote for self-pity. It takes thoughts off oneself, but more important, it helps the person find opportunity to invest himself or herself in others and to find meaning in life.

10. Don't tell anybody else what the person said to you. Confidentiality is a must unless you are seeking help for your counseling from a professional. In this case, it is not gossip but a professional consultation.

11. If major problems occur, refer the person to the pastor, to his or her physician, or to another appropriate professional.

Helping Children Mourn

I had an illuminating experience when my daughter Ruth was 3½ years old. From it derive several of the suggestions which follow. My wife and I brought her with us to a funeral home where an elderly friend's body lay in state. My daughter had not met the man; so there was minimal emotional involvement. But to the extent that mental and subconscious processes apply to grief, her experience is revealing. As my wife and I viewed the man's body in the casket, Ruth said, "Let me see in there." I picked her up, and she asked, "Is he sleeping?" "No," I replied, "he is dead." Her mother replied, "He looks like he is sleeping, but he is not breathing. There is no life in him." This satisfied Ruth, and she asked to be put down. After we had talked with several family members, Ruth said to her mother, "I want to see the man." Her mother picked her up, and viewing him again, Ruth asked, "Who shot him?" Up to this time Ruth's experience with death had been via TV where frequently people die young and violently. "No one shot him," replied her mother. "He was an old man, and his body wore out."

"Where are his feet?" she asked next.

"They are under that part of the casket," replied my wife,

pointing to the enclosed portion. This satisfied Ruth, and she squirmed down to the floor. At that moment the man's widow came in the door, and Ruth, knowing her as a friend, ran up to her, kissed her, and said, "A man died." She then ran back to her mother.

As we left in the car, my wife made a comment about our friend's hospitalization. Ruth asked, "Where did he die?"

"In the hospital," responded her mother.

"Daddy's hospital?"

"Yes," I said.

For the first time a strong emotion appeared in Ruth's speech, and she said, "I don't want to talk about it *anymore!*"

In the experience of this encounter we make our first point: avoid confusing adult meanings of death with those the child has in mind. That our friend had his feet in death was a real concern for Ruth. And how could we know that she thought everybody died by being shot?

We know the comfort of the adult meaning of life after death, but the child only knows that his or her emotional support is gone. To tell the child that Jesus or God has taken the loved one is to give opportunity for intellectual misunderstanding and emotional resentment of God and Jesus for taking away someone the child still needs. God does take us, but we should explain that his taking someone is an expression of God's love for us when the body "wears out."

It is preferable that we talk with the child about those subjects which he or she introduces. This is where the child is in his or her grief. These may be biological concerns, as with my daughter, or the religious-philosophical-emotional concern of a teenager who already knows the biological answers.

Funerals and rituals are our way of saying emotional good-byes to people important to us. Children should have the benefit of these rites, but they should also be protected from rituals that become too emotional for their immature personalities. My wife and I, in looking back over this experience, think it was good for our daughter to experience people grieving over a loss. It was a helpful corrective to television murder mysteries in which people are treated as worthless, expendable objects. Perhaps our society does too good a job of shielding children from the experiences of death.

When the man's death was associated with "Daddy's hospital" and Daddy, my daughter felt threatened. She handled the threat by closing the conversation. In such a situation be generous with reassurances and support.

"Daddy, are you going to die?" This question was asked by the daughter of a friend. The friend reasoned that, according to the insurance company's actuary, he had many years of life and replied, "Not for a long time." The answer was designed to reassure the daughter that her dad would not die *soon.* Sometimes the reassurance comes through the special efforts to be close. This can be achieved in playing games, having a "midnight snack" together, going on a bike ride. More is involved in these experiences than the words in a counseling situation. Companionship, the gift of one's whole person, is the blessing which makes the grief-stricken one whole.

Grief is a Pandora's box of guilt, uncertainty, fear, and anxiety. For the child, support and reassurance come from relationships with strong adults who are calm and secure. When the parent cannot be this to the child, he or she should acknowledge it to himself or herself and, for the sake of the child, seek helping relationships with a minister or friends.

Next, when a child is not facing loss redemptively, one can help by initiating an encounter. A good way is with the open-ended question, such as "What are your thoughts about Dad's (or pet's) death?" or "Why do you think grandmother (or the pet) died?" or "Are there any questions you want to ask me about the funeral?" These general questions give the child a chance to reveal his or her true feelings and thoughts. This is in contrast to some questions which would lead the child to give answers he or she thinks you want.

Another important point is: don't push the child to talk about death. You may open the conversation, but don't push too hard. If the child refuses to face death with you, perhaps you can find someone else who will help you with facilitating the child's grief work. It may be that the child senses something in you and intuitively knows he cannot receive help until you get some help with your grief.

Do not, however, hide the fact of death from a child. If parents don't tell about a relative's death, other children or adults will accidently tell. Then the child will not feel free to talk about it with you. Death cannot be hidden, and to deny knowledge of it is deceitful. It is an unsuccessful way of handling the problem and is potentially harmful.

Make sure what you say to a child is true. Honesty in facts and feelings is always in season. "White lies," half-truths, and deceptions can be deeply set by strong emotions and hard to overcome later in life.

Finally, resist efforts to develop intellectual substitutes for deep emotions and to intellectualize and rationalize grief. We have a long child-rearing tradition of suppressing strong "negative" emotions, especially in boys. A grieving child should be *seen and heard.* Loss is certain. Death is for all of us. But life for the survivors must and will go on. The quality of that life is enhanced as He who gives us eternal life also reaches into our lives with redemptive fellowships, both human and divine. These relationships contain the gift of resources which permit life to be lived abundantly, that is, "pulled together" again—*religio.*

4

The ABC's of Institutional Visitation: Hospital and Nursing Home

The world of institutional caring and healing is a subworld within our larger world. It is peopled with drama; its own clock knows no off-hours nor rest periods. Its rules and assumptions are alien culture to many patients and visitors.

Maybe you are an official visitor in a hospital from your church, or you are visiting a friend. But whether you are a relative or a close or casual friend, you are still a visitor. The patient's room is to be considered as private as the home, and unless you are visiting your husband, wife, dependent child, or aged parent, it would be best if you consider yourself a guest. It may be that you approach the door, feeling uncomfortable and uncertain as to how you will find the patient. The suggestions which follow are offered to make your visit as helpful as possible.

FOCUS UPON THE ENVIRONMENT

A seminary professor said: "You will be asked to pray in public, and at times there will be no opportunity to prepare. In order to pray a good pastoral prayer without preparation, keep the five fingers of prayer in your thoughts: adoration, confession, intercession, petition, and dedication." This advice has been followed and proved helpful. When visiting in the hospital, keep in your mind's consciousness four objects: focus upon the environment of the room, the patient, yourself, and your purpose.

Time Factors

What time of day is best? Hospital visiting hours are for visiting purposes. Other hours are for treatment and rest. Try not to visit at mealtimes. But if you *must* visit during lunch hour or if you *must* be there at a meal, insist that the patient continue with his or her meal. Not all institutional cooking is as good as home cooking. Even a hot, deliciously prepared meal turned cold is not a good meal. Also, when someone is in the hospital, the illness itself, depression, or some medication may be such that the patient has no appetite. Don't give the patient an excuse not to take that essential physical nourishment. But best of all, go during visiting hours only. Major treatments, baths, baby feedings, etc., are usually done at the No Visiting times, and this is the reason for No Visitors times. You aren't being smart by slipping in the back door during this period. Exceptions to this rule are made for the minister. Quite often, when there are emotional moods that are depressing to the individual or when the life stresses have been such that they have affected the individual's health, the minister can, by using his good judgment, be quite helpful during these No Visiting hours. He knows that he will not be disturbed by a visitor walking in the door, and he can sometimes render his most effective ministry if uninterrupted. But this privilege probably will not be extended to lay-shepherding visitors.

Presurgical visits are often more effective the day before surgery. Studies of anxiety levels and other factors have shown this to be true.[1]

How long should your visit last? Normally limit it to about five to ten minutes. Visits tire the patient, especially those people who are weak from surgery or prolonged illness. If the patient wishes you to stay longer than five minutes, he or she will say so with conviction. If you have any sensitivity at all to the moods in a person's voice, you will know if he or she really wants you to stay. If the patient offers a polite invitation to stay longer, take it as a courtesy and come another time. He or she will thank you for hearing the real message, the message in the tone of voice rather than the message in the words. How long you stay in a room is usually determined by your closeness to the patient, his or her physical and emotional condition at the time, and the purpose of your visit. To some patients, we are a necessary source of strength; to others, a good friend who wears like an old shoe; and to other patients, we are guests who must be entertained. So judge your visits accordingly. There's no rule of thumb on how long to stay that can be applied to all situations. This is a matter for your personal judgment. Finally, leave when you say you are leaving.

At the Door

As you arrive at the door, you may find it closed. You will knock for permission to enter. One day I was visiting in the hospital and found a large sign on a woman's door. It read: "Knock for permission to enter, not to announce that you are coming in." The door may be closed because some intimate treatment is being given, or the patient may be sleeping or in a great deal of pain and just doesn't want the stimulation of another individual.

Or you may appear at the door and the nurse call light is lit. Check with the nurse before you enter. The light is on because the patient wants some service performed. Wait until the need is met before entering. If you are in doubt of the appropriateness of a visit at that time, check with the nursing station.

Please note carefully the No Visitors and Isolation signs. One day a visitor was caught in a room with an isolated patient. He did not have on the necessary protective clothing and mask, and he had to wait for more than an hour before being cleared to leave the room. Frequently people in isolation are lonely; call them on the telephone if their condition permits such a call. If a No Visitors sign is posted, then sign your name or leave a note—a note that says something very special about how you are feeling toward the patient. It will mean much more than just your name.

When you do knock, do so gently. The patient may be asleep, but a family member may be awake and will answer. Sometimes the patient will want to be awakened. This is especially so if the daytime sleep interferes with sleeping at night. But check with the family on the advisability of waking the patient.

The Environment in the Room

Be aware of the condition of the other patients if you are visiting in a semiprivate room or ward. Your friend may be fine, but the other patient may be very ill. Try to keep others' needs in mind.

No gang visiting, that is, no more than two or three visitors at a time. The stimulation of a large group of cheerful helpers is often too much good at one time. It is possible for so many people to overwhelm the emotional capacity of the patient. If others are present in the room, you can note the fact and offer to come back. It may be that the people visiting before you will want to use your visit as an opportunity to terminate theirs.

No smoking, please. Fresh air is important to health. The patient may be taking oxygen, and the flame from a cigarette lighter could cause an explosion. Or the doctor may have the patient restricted from smoking, and your cigarette is too much of a temptation. Sometimes breathing treatments such as fogging are used. Also, chronic lung disorders can be irritated by the toxic cigarette fumes. For all these reasons—please, no smoking.

FOCUS UPON THE PATIENT

Now that you're in the room, take a position in line with the patient's vision, expecially if his or her position on the bed is limited by traction, sandbags, etc. Or perhaps the person has had surgery and has been placed in a certain postion for a specified length of time. It is easier for you to move around so that the patient can see you than for the patient to move.

Do not lean, touch, or sit on the bed, especially if the patient has had surgery. Not only do stitches pull and incisions hurt, but you could introduce germs that can be transmitted to the patient.

Always let the patient offer to shake hands with you. Someone has called "king arthritis" a tyrant. Also, the patient's hand may be sore from an intravenous injection, or it may be tender from other causes. Let the warmth of your greeting be conveyed through your smile, voice, and general manner.

During the visit, if the person uses you as a counselor to help with a problem and if the catharsis of feelings is upsetting the patient emotionally and physically, convey to him or her that this is happening, stop it, and offer to talk about the problem later when the person is calmer. If you feel the patient needs a more experienced counselor, convey this belief to him or her. If you promise to talk about this later, be sure you do so.

Use prayer when it is requested or according to your religious tradition. Prayers should be specific and positive. We have much for which to be grateful and need to concentrate upon God's resources which heal and sustain us. Pray for the family. Pray for God's human healing servants—the doctor, hospital staff, and the ministers. Prayers, in general, should be short. (For more on this, see chapter 7).

Keep bad reports about mutual friends' accidents and deaths to a minimum. Timing bad news should be a matter of personal judgment, perhaps in consultation with the head nurse and the doctor. Because we love, we are concerned about others, and most patients have enough personal concern and pain without other people's problems being introduced. Don't argue about politics or controversial issues. You may be prophetic and have God's latest word on a social issue, but wait until the patient is well before you spring the truth on him or her. Practice Ecclesiastes 3:1, "For everything there is a season, and a time. . . ." One of those times is a time to heal.

Consider the possible effect of whispering upon the patient, and you will conclude that whispering in the room to other visitors is a strict "no-no." Many patients are suspicious in this day when so much information about medical conditions is withheld. One patient said, "While you are waiting for tests to be read, you imagine a thousand things, and they are all bad." The "sleeping" patient may be playing the ancient game of "possum," or his sleep may be fitful. A patient wrote me a letter upon returning home after having spent several days in our intensive care unit. He had read in the paper an article which I had written: "How to Pray with Those Who Are Ill." He said, "You are right when you said that the sense of hearing is the last sense to be retained. I heard everything that went on around me." Each situation must be judged on its own merits, but many patients are fearful of knowing the truth. The truth may be too much for them to bear emotionally at that particular time, and they will imagine the worst when there is whispering.

Offer medical information sparingly. Never destroy the patient's faith in his doctor or the hospital staff. Each person's treatment is tailor-made for his condition, and often there is more than one prescribed treatment for an illness. The patient could have a second illness such as diabetes or some other complication which would dictate a different form of treatment than what you had for that same illness. I well remember that one day I went to a patient's room, and the woman in the bed said, "Chaplain, I understand you had the same illness that I have." She continued, "How long did it take you to get over your illness?" I told her truthfully that it took me forty days. And abruptly she sat upright in bed and exclaimed, "Forty days!" I had to say, "Hold it! I had some complications which you do not have. Just because it took me that long to get well is no sign it will take you that long." Reassuring words are helpful when people begin to express their fears about their condition and are comparing themselves with somebody else who got over that condition in three days, while they're going on three weeks with theirs. When we were children, we played doctor and nurse. That's fine; that's what we are supposed to do while we are children—try out adult roles. But when we go to visit the hospital, we are not there to play the children's game of doctor and nurse. So don't pick it up again. Let me emphasize: Never destroy the patient's faith in the doctor or in the hospital staff. Patients must place their trust in these individuals, and trust is a necessary spiritual strength. We must not destroy patients' trust in their doctors.

Don't ask the diagnosis. It could be embarrassing! Instead, ask how things are going, or use some other general opener.

Last but not least, observe signs of discomfort: bed sheets disarrayed, body movements, facial tension, comments by the patient ("I need a shot for pain." "I've just had a shot," etc.), uneaten food on meal trays, sleepiness, pulleys for traction, etc.

FOCUS UPON YOURSELF

Be relaxed. If you're tired or depressed or sick yourself, postpone the visit. Perhaps a telephone call to the person's house or a note would say to this individual that "You are not forgotten; I do love you, but I'm just not able to be there myself right now and be the kind of visitor you need." Be cheerful, but don't force cheerfulness if you don't feel it. Often during illness we are very sensitive to the moods of others and more susceptible to "catching" their moods than when we are normally strong. Use humor if you think it's appropriate. But please, no belly-shaking jokes for at least ten days after surgery! This is just a simple reality that so many people forget. One good rule is to enter the room with a neutral-mood tone—no excessive joy or sympathy. It is better for you to adjust to the patient's mood than for him or her to adjust to yours.

Let your laughter and voice level be consistent with the person's hearing ability. Note hearing aids; it is appropriate to ask a person wearing a hearing aid if your voice level is okay. Once while visiting, I did not see the patient's hearing aid because of the way his head was turned. But it was obvious that he wasn't hearing me talking in that volume of voice, so I raised my voice considerably, and he *still* couldn't hear me. He then turned his head slightly, and I saw the hearing aid. I adjusted my volume and said, "Can you hear me when I talk at this voice level?" He said, "Yes," but his hearing aid was rather selective in its pickup. I suspect his problem was tone, not volume deafness. It is a common mistake to talk too loudly to someone wearing a hearing aid. Slow speech spoken forcefully sometimes is effective in communicating. We should also add that in times of sickness and emotional distress, the ability to tolerate noise is lessened, and loud talking can irritate and fatigue the patient.

"Listen"—note your own feelings. Are you anxious, bored, or angry? These feelings tell you how you are reacting emotionally to the situation. Or they may be the feelings of the patient resonating in you.

Remember you are the patient's *guest,* and your visit is for *his* or *her* benefit, not yours.

Don't talk about intimate aspects of your visit to others. You need the reputation of being someone "safe to talk to." Gossiping can also destroy a visitation ministry and/or the visitor's ministry.

As a general rule, you should listen more than you talk. But don't demand that the patient carry the major responsibility for the conversation. The patient's physical and emotional condition are two major variables here. Another variable is the visitor's personal knowledge of the patient. That is, the visitor and the sick patient may be good friends, and this fact may cause a tiring, too lengthy, visit. There are many factors which enter into a visit, but in summary, the "listening ministry" frequently is as much an intitution—an art—as it is a science.

FOCUS UPON YOUR PURPOSE

A lay shepherd said, "I'm not sure we should have a visitation group." A doctor sent a message to me through my wife: "Tell your husband to teach his course on hospital visitation and then tell them not to visit. Patients are too sick to entertain visitors." I agree with the doctor on the last point. Most patients *are* too sick to entertain. But our business is not to be entertained or to socialize. Also, a hospitalized patient's need for a supportive community does not cease upon admission; rather, it *increases* during a crisis. Our responsibility as the church is to meet that need in the wisest, most helpful way possible. How do we justify such a ministry? The answer is to be found in the purpose of lay visitation. Is it valid? What distinguishes a lay shepherd's visit from a social call made by another church visitor who wants to do something "nice"?

Shepherding, in the Judeo-Christian faiths, is more than a social call extending "best wishes." The lay shepherd's visit is one with an offer to help, to go the second mile. It is an offering of oneself, one's compassion, time, and talents. It is a ministry of the church symbolized in the witness of you, the visitor. One would hope that Christian theology, crisis theory, and visitation principles, plus the ongoing fellowship of the lay-shepherding group itself, will make an improvement in the quality of visits. Also, the goal of harmonizing the visitation with other healing helpers will contribute to the realization of a holistic approach to Christian healing. Healing is more than body repair work.

One purpose may be to render a physical service: feed the patient, monitor visitor traffic, answer the telephone, or assist the family. As a result of practical experience and observation, your intended purpose may change when you arrive at the patient's room.

Your purpose is directly related to the patient's need. For example, your intended purpose was to visit a depressed patient. But you find the patient alone, with a temperature and covered with sweat. Instead of making a cheering visit, you will instead inform the nurse of the problem and request that the patient's pajamas and sheets be changed.

And finally, visitation ministry establishes rapport. This rapport will be valuable in the important ministry of posthospitalization and/or supportive ministry. You are laying the foundation for a posthospitalization ministry by how you relate as a lay shepherd to the hospitalized person. And this latter ministry may prove more valuable than the initial visits in the hospital.

As a check on the effectiveness of my doctor of ministry project, the lay shepherds' visits to the hospitalized were followed by a questionnaire filled out by the patient. I found this to be true: *Laity do not fulfill the same ministry to the sick as does the pastor. There is overlap, but both pastor and laity meet specific needs of a fellowship and supportive nature not met by the other.* The lay shepherd communicated an additional spiritual concern and ministry by the church which was not communicated by a casual visit from a friend. The lay shepherd's ministry communicated the same love and concern of personal friends, but that love was in the meaningful context of spiritual service which was noted with appreciation by the hospitalized persons.

The pastor's visits were more spiritually and personally intimate and took the form of professional ministry. He or she was seen in the symbolic role of God's shepherd. In conclusion, I recommended lay visitation as a ministry which meets definite needs not met by pastors and personal friends.

Visitation is a ministry of love. It fulfills the Second Commandment of Jesus that we love our neighbor as ourselves. In addition, we are asked in the Epistle of James to visit the sick. If we do so with wisdom and love, then our visits will be appreciated, helpful, and remembered for a long time.

THE ABC'S OF NURSING HOME VISITATION

Much that has been said about hospital visitation applies to nursing-home visitation. Keep in the mind's eye four things: environment, resident, self, and purpose. But there are other factors to consider.

Many nursing-home residents have *no* home or cannot return to their homes. They are lonely, cut off from the essential nourishment given by a "place," their *own* place. Depression is common; hopelessness can be a fatal disease of the spirit. Great frustration is experienced as a result of the restrictive limits imposed by the weak and sick body and the nursing home environment. Many residents view the nursing home as the last stop on a one-way trip to death. They give up, seeing no possibility of a return to their former independent life-style. It should come as no surprise that the physical, emotional, and social shocks are more than the weakened person can take, and death overtakes many residents during their first year in the "home." In such an environmental and personal context, visits can be longer. There should also be advance prayer and planning before the visit. Advance notice to the nursing-home staff may be necessary, especially if they must assist the resident with personal grooming.

Visits at mealtimes may be appropriate. Check with the nursing home. In addition to all the reasons given for hospital eating problems, we can add oral and dental problems. For many people, the meal was a family and social happy hour. A visit could help rekindle those past happy times.

Should the visit be a ministry to a large group of residents, have the occasion placed on the nursing home's social calendar. In discussing lay shepherding with Savannah, Georgia, nursing-home administrators and activities directors, a problem emerged: fear of the residents. Many groups bring programs, but a great need is the person-to-person conversation. The nursing home officials say, "Don't run away after the program! Visit person-to-person. It makes a difference in their lives!"

An "Adopt a Grandparent" program can be helpful to those residents who have outlived their families or who have no immediate family. This could be taken as a project by a Sunday school class. As a pastor, I have heard several elderly persons say that they had served their church faithfully when they were in their prime, but now the church had forgotten them. This should not be!

If you take small children with you, remember that their energy and activity make older people nervous. Grandchildren bless their grandparents twice: once when they come and again when they leave!

An especially acute problem is seen in the elderly, especially nursing-home residents. Many of them suffer from brain deterioration and a decrease in mental functioning. It is recommended that the visitor "check out" damaging "information," such as abuse or neglect of residents, before announcing the alleged problem to the public. No one is perfect in care giving, and misinformation spread abroad is damaging to residents, family, and staff.

Two small children were talking. One asked, "Why does your grandmother read the Bible so much? "She is preparing for finals," replied the second child. "Religion and old age go together," said one nursing-home administrator. Worship services and prayer groups are very important. But they can be abused by pushy, poorly informed people who believe that their understanding of faith is the *only* way to respond to God's love. Their intolerance is self-judgment when seen in the light of Christian love (1 Corinthians 13) which is basic to all our denominational practices.

Physical ministry is a great need. Residents need hairdressers, crafts instruction, occupational and physical therapy aids, to name a few. It would be easy to continue in this manner of suggesting "please do's" and "no-no's." This would amount to a legalistic approach to care. Instead, seek the guidance of the Holy Spirit. Pray and plan your visits ahead, and be alert and flexible during visits, and visit with nursing-home staff. They can tell you of needs, and you can bless their lives, too.

5
Hope and Healing

Hope is a powerful ingredient in spiritual therapy, especially in relation to depression and despair. Indeed, someone has called despair an "illness of hope." Hope is a balm of comfort from the past. It is an assurance that God will bless us in the present and an assurance that relief and good are provided for our future.

HOPE AS PAST EXPERIENCE

The first thing to note about hope is that it is rooted in the past. All of us have a history of what God has already done for us or for someone close to us. This history justifies and gives us the opportunity to intervene in the life of a person we wish to help. The recollection of this personal spiritual history has the effect of strengthening hope. A simple technique is to help the patient recall personal experiences of the past in which things looked hopeless, in which there were great crises and trauma in his or her life. At that time God came through with grace sufficient for the person's needs. Faith reasons that God, who was faithful in the past, will be faithful in the present. The person of faith can count upon his wisdom, love, and power to work out the best in this current difficult situation.

At the same time it may be appropriate for you, the helper, to recall personal experiences in which God has been of help to you. But before you share, ask yourself, "How appropriate is *my* story to this person's needs?" All of this recalling of personal experiences, whether it be your own or the patient's, should be done with caution and compassion. If you use this technique, be brief in the recall. And expect some people to resent it.

Research conducted by Dr. C. P. Richter with rats produced an unexpected insight into hope as a learning experience. Rats placed in a jar of water quickly gave up swimming and died. However, those rats which were removed several times (rescued), when returned to the water, evidently viewed their own situation with hope and would remain swimming for many hours, sustained by their experiences of rescue. Dr. Paul Pruyser summarized the phenomenon as follows: "One little ray of hope in a world of darkness is enough to invigorate some people. One moment of release from unbearable stress makes the world appear in a different image." [1]

HOPE AS A FUTURE-ORIENTED EXPERIENCE

The second thing we can say of hope is that it is future oriented. It looks forward to a better world than this one. But it also looks forward to a better tomorrow in this world. Paul, following the example of Jesus, helps us with this dimension of hope. In his letter to the Christians in Rome he says:

> I consider that the sufferings of this present time are not worth comparing to the glory that is to be revealed to us. For the creation waits with eager longing for the revealing of the sons of God; for the creation was subjected to futility, not of its own will but by the will of him who subjected it in hope; because the creation itself will be set free from its bondage to decay and obtain the glorious liberty of the children of God. We know that the whole creation has been groaning in travail together until now; and not only the creation, but we ourselves, who have the first fruits of the Spirit, groan inwardly as we wait for adoption as sons, the redemption of our bodies. For in this hope we were saved. Now hope that is seen is not hope. For who hopes for what he sees? But if we hope for what we do not see, we wait for it with patience (Romans 8:18-25).

For our purpose, the importance of this Scripture on hope is in the twenty-third verse where it reads "first fruits." The first fruits have to do with the harvest of crops. The phrase refers to the initial ripening of wheat, apples, etc. These first fruits belong to God. They are taken to the temple and sacrificed to God. The coming of the first fruits tells us that the ripening process has begun and that, therefore, we can anticipate our harvest.

When applied to Christians, it means that we are now able to experience the powers of the kingdom of heaven. And among the influences upon our present-day life are spiritual blessings, including healing and the guidance our lives must receive . Or to use Paul again, we experience the fruits and gifts of the Holy Spirit in our daily activities. With only this small amount of spiritual experience, Paul says we are justified in hoping for a kingdom, existing now, but which will be experienced fully beyond the present bodily life.

This hope has a practical consequence. It helps if we compare our present suffering with the partially experienced future hope. Such a comparison strengthens us in the present stressful times! "I consider that the sufferings of this present time are not worth comparing with the glory that is to be revealed to us" (Romans 8:18). Hope has the additional practical consequence of mobilizing our personal resources, and it creates a receptive attitude to help from others and God.

Again the scientific study of hope confirms this Christian insight of hope as a dynamic future-oriented process:

> An important step in the development of overcoming despair is the point at which the patient exchanges his static goal in life for a growing and moving one. Usually the goal has been perceived as a static, utopian state—"and they were married and lived happily ever after." It is much more realistic and helpful, however, to view it as a dynamic process of reception, expression, action, searching, growing.[2]

HOPE AS PRESENT EXPERIENCE

We have said that hope is rooted in past experiences and is future oriented. Now look at hope as a present experience.

Paul says to us that the kingdom is present and that it can be experienced in the present life. It would follow that if we can recognize the budding gifts and fruits of hope, this can help us raise the present experiences of hope. One way of doing this is by *offering oneself as a helper*. We offer our acceptance of the person as he or she *is;* we offer our love, our skills in relationship, and our time to listen. Hope is found in an interpersonal process.

> Marcel stresses that true hoping requires an inter-personal context. . . . Isolation leads to hopelessness and to disintegration of personality functioning. When communication between persons fails, the isolated individual goes to pieces. . . . Who gives hope to whom is an irrelevant question; the point is that hoping is generated *in* the relationship.[3]

The second helpful ministry proceeds from the first: *help the person accept himself or herself and his or her altered self-image.* Somehow, it seems that when other people accept us as we are, our view of ourselves is affected, and we are better able to accept ourselves. This is especially true if surgery or an illness, such as a stroke or an injury that has cut the spinal cord has greatly altered one's self-image.

We may also raise the present-day level and experience of hope by *addressing the matter of personal goals.* Explore with the patient the possibility and consequences of lowering the rehabilitation goals. If the person is under the care of a professional therapist or a doctor, check with the professional rehabilitation worker or encourage the person to do this. It may also be helpful to lengthen the time needed to reach these goals, or perhaps a combination of the two is required. To repeat (and thus stress), if the person is receiving continuing therapy, the therapist should be involved in all decisions.

Another way of helping is also related to rehabilitation goals and purposes, namely, *helping the person find new goals and purposes for living.* He or she may never be able to achieve the previously set marks of achievement, nor may the person ever be able to render the great services of his or her previous vision. New dreams must be dreamed. New goals, probably including vocational ones, must be discovered. This is not an easy task nor one hastily accomplished. One person who had a stroke said to me, "I am my wife's automatic dishwasher." Here was something he could do for his wife who was having to do so much for him. This woman still had her husband and his companionship and thoughtfulness. And dishwashing was a symbol of his love for her and of his will to live and to contribute as much as possible. A person may no longer be able to move mountains, but may now merely be able only to kick over and dust poison on anthills. The important point is that goals in the future must be "deeply important to the patient."[4]

The lay shepherd should also *point out that achieving results in therapy is a mark of the presence of God and an occasion for hope.* Let us imagine a person who has had a stroke. One day he begins to wiggle the end of a finger, or feeling returns. These small evidences of the return of bodily functions have a tremendous bearing upon one's spirit. For if this little has happened, *maybe* much more can be achieved! Occupational therapy, speech therapy, and physical therapy, as they help the person regain lost functions, also affect his spirit and his sense of hope.

> Nothing is so inducive to hoping as one hope that was fulfilled. For hoping does not merely deal with possibilities, but also with the realization of possibilities. Tension between the actual and the possible is the climate in which hoping can thrive.[5]

A positive technique for raising the present-day level and experience of hope is through the *discovering of resources.* There are personal resources. Focus upon the abilities that remain. The tendency is to focus upon the problems, to look at them and gaze at them and think about them and worry about them until we have depressed ourselves. It is much better to discover and concentrate upon the personal resources instead of pathology. The owner of a small business, in a moment of depression, was ready to sell his business and sit in his rocking chair until he died. The chaplain asked him to shift his thoughts from his paralysis and fears to his remaining strengths. He could write his signature, thus making his decisions legal; his business knowledge was intact, and he was in good physical condition except for the stroke damage. It was pointed out that he could "hire a pair of legs and arms" (a handyman) to do the physical parts of the job, while he continued to make the decisions. This change in focus to strengths was quickly followed by a lifting of the man's depression.

> To the hoper, reality is not fixed and crystallized, but open ended. And with that, the hoping person assumes that reality has resources which are as yet undiscovered and untapped. In hoping, one lives life as adventure.[6]

Other resources are found in the family. Who is the family encourager? Who is the strong planner? Who has the bulldog attitude that forces results when all timid-hearted souls have given up long ago? Blessed are those who have either a strong wife or husband or child who is able to come through with the motivational strengths that only a family can offer.

Look to the community for its resources. This includes both private and government sectors. There are many private agencies sponsored by individuals, churches, or United Community Services, as well as many government agencies. Quite frequently a social worker can be very helpful, and the patient might best be referred to a social worker to find out what services are available. Does your church have a talent or vocational file? Perhaps an active or retired social worker would welcome this opportunity to serve.

Religious resources must be discovered and used. There are personal religious experiences which have been mentioned earlier in regard to hope being a past experience. These can be recalled; indeed, the Psalms utilize this technique (Psalms 42:4-5; 44:1; 116). Also, this is one of the purposes of worship and preaching: to relive— experience today—the reality of past salvation experiences with God. There are the resources of the organized church. The church fellowship is called a family, and brothers and sisters in Christ can be of help.

Raising the present-day experience of hope is also achieved by *answering religious and philosophical questions*. Essential to this endeavor is our concept of God. If our image of God is that of an avenging, punishing deity, then it is less likely that we will be helped as much as we would be by the concept of deity as one who loves us. A biblical scholar has said that the name God revealed to Moses in the wilderness, *YAHWEH,* should be translated "God is for us" or "I am for you." Here the emphasis is not upon the idea of substance (that is, what God is made of), or pure being, namely "I am," which has been a traditional interpretation (Exodus 3:6). But, rather, it is more like the Hebrew concept of God that is seen throughout the Bible, namely *God in action blessing his people.* Even Paul said, "If God is for us . . ." (Romans 8:31).

Another important idea in our concept of God is *Emmanuel—* "God is with us." We see this experience of "God being with us" in the Bible. It is seen most clearly in Jesus' ministry. "Believe me that I am in the Father and the Father in me" (John 14:11). This "being with" or incarnation shows the intimacy of spiritual community. Jesus' prayer in John 17 is a promise of continued spiritual intimacy with its comfort. (See also the message of intimacy and hope in Psalm 131.)

Other religious and philosophical questions may be: "Does God will evil?" "Why does God permit evil?" "Why me? I try to live a good life."

Another way of raising the present-day level of hope is in *helping the person establish a spirit of receptivity, that is, of receiving, being patient, being willing to wait.* Our American society has taught us well how to work. We have conquered a continent. It is part of our tradition to work hard to overcome. We call it the "Protestant work ethic." In a distortion of this important value, we see this drive to work being expressed in the "illness" or anxiety of a person who doesn't know what to do with Sunday, hence the motivation to make Sunday like any other day of work.

But if we work, we must also rest. If we are to continue to give, we must learn to receive. There is a rhythm in life of working and waiting, of giving and getting. And sometimes helping a person with a serious illness involves helping him establish this rhythm in life. Confirmation of this balanced dual need comes from medical research in brain hemisphere dominance.[7]

Last but not least, we can raise the present level of hope by *helping the person accept the responsibility to help himself or herself.* "You can't learn anybody anything." You may teach, but you can't make a person learn. Clearly, even our language portrays this truth about ourselves: *We must possess the will to help ourselves.* Nobody can do it for us. Some help isn't helpful, but not because it is not appropriate. It may be very appropriate, but it is not helpful because it is not received or wanted.

The will to assume responsibility to help oneself can frequently be greatly lowered by a lack of hope. And if we are successful in raising the present-day level of the experience of hope, we will discover that assuming responsibility is a blessing which grows with use. As we experience hope, one of its blessings is the strengthening of the will to help oneself.

The experience of hoping presupposes the experience of doubting, fearing and despairing. Hoping is not an elegant drifting in leisure and comfort, as a tourist may do in a Venetian gondola. It is much more like steering a ship in a gale. Hoping is a singulary unsentimental and unromantic affair. It permits no departure from reality, otherwise it becomes illusion and delusion.[8]

One danger in mobilizing hope must be noted: promising too much success. Do not encourage the setting of too high goals. It would be better to err on the conservative side and overachieve than to fall far short of an unrealistically high goal. Hopes crushed to earth do not always rise again. To minimize this danger, hope mobilizing is best done in cooperation with doctors and paramedical personnel, such as vocational, physical, and speech therapists. Indeed, these are ideal hope counselors, for they add to their professional skills the healing power of hope. But often these professional persons may not be adequate, or the ill person may need additional helpers. In this case the *established* relationships of a pastor, family, and friends—including lay shepherds—may be the factor which makes hope succeed. In this multiple approach of professionals and volunteers we see the promise of Proverbs 11:14 fulfilled: "In an abundance of counselors there is safety."

There is frequently a crisis in hope when the longed-for physical recovery is not achieved. The movie *The Robe* has a moving scene in which a paralyzed woman's attitude toward her illness was beautifully victorious. She had seen Jesus but was still paralyzed. When asked why Jesus did not heal her, she replied that he had healed her attitude toward her illness. For her, this was the greater need, and Jesus saw it and gave her what she needed most. Furthermore, her situation was a message that misfortune need not deprive anyone of happiness in his kingdom.

> I walked a mile with Pleasure;
> She chattered all the way,
> But left me none the wiser
> For all she had to say.
>
> I walked a mile with Sorrow
> And ne'er a word said she;

62 □ Lay Shepherding

But oh, the things I learned from her
When Sorrow walked with me!
"Along the Road"
Robert Browning Hamilton

Dr. Lawrence LeShan, in commenting upon therapy that increased the will to live in the terminal patient, says that in his or her growth, self-exploration, and self-acceptance, the patient becomes a fuller person. He suggests that counseling should concentrate more "on the expansion and freeing of the self than on physical recovery."[9] This goal is valid for those whose prognosis is good but who need hope to maximize physical recovery and self-image.

For many people, acceptance of a permanent disability and an attitude that seeks to utilize the disability for good is the highest possible goal. This goal is not a "sour grapes" attitude or thinking. Hope for physical healing may not be realized, but neither should a victorious attitude be minimized. Paul was not healed of his thorn in the flesh. He was told by God, "My grace is sufficient for you" (2 Corinthians 12:9). Indeed, wounded healers are sometimes more effective than those who have no scars.

There is one additional experience in which our hope appears not to be answered affirmatively. Sometimes our hope for continued life is not answered. A frequent experience encountered with elderly people is "giving up." This is seen most often following surgery or the death of a spouse. Sometimes our best efforts do not prevail, and with a deep sense of helplessness we watch the person sink into lethargy or a coma and leave this life. Always our prayer is, "God's will be done." God is for us, and he is with us. Then, of all times, we must trust him. The beginning and end of life are clouded in mystery. That is something we must accept.

Faith, hope, and love must always be held in the context of Jesus' resurrection and the promise of our own resurrection. Job asked if a person's hope dies as persons die (Job 17:13-16). Paul answered with the message that it is eternal (1 Corinthians 13:13). As we experience hope in the present day, it says to us that these kingdom gifts are the first fruits which we shall know in all of the fullness of harvest in the life beyond this one. God has given us the mission of strengthening the experience of these first fruits in the lives of his people who need the power of a vision of hope for today.

6

Listening That Develops Wholeness

THE PARTS OF THE COMMUNICATION PROCESS

Blessed are you if you receive the compliment "You are an easy person to talk to." There are effective ways of listening and obviously ineffective ways, since we also hear negative evaluations, such as "He's a fine person (preacher, doctor, etc.), but you have to stand on his toes to make him listen. What I said went in one ear and out the other!" Awareness of the parts of the communication process facilitates redemptive listening.

Word symbols are the most obvious parts of communication, but they are not all the message and may not be the important part of the message; or they may be a conscious or subconscious effort to disguise the real message. As we listen to the words, we need to ask ourselves what they convey by way of facts and feelings. They may contain the intellectual content and may be emotionally neutral, or more likely, they will reveal the emotional involvement of the person. A father said one day, "There's going to be a wedding at our house." These words can be said with different emotions. They can be read joyfully, for example, or in a way which is emotionally neutral. But the father in this actual case was domineering and did not like the bridegroom; the important message was in the emotion and was his displeasure over the wedding at his home!

Another part of the communication is *nonverbal symbols*. These symbols convey rational messages as well as all of the emotions experienced by people. Some of the emotional "symbols" are: anger, gratitude, guilt, seduction, etc. One's emotions are also communicated through facial expressions, including skin changes—flushes and loss of color. Nonverbal communication includes the manner of dress, physical appearance, mannerisms, or repetitive behavior in body language. Body language to watch for includes fidgeting, twitching of eyelids, trembling lips, and especially the use of the eyes.

A third important part of the communication process is *silence*. Some silence is empty. It reveals a mind out of gear. Reasons for empty silence include fatigue, a need to withdraw, or irresponsibility. Silence may be a deliberate cloak to conceal, or the person may have said more than he or she planned. The speaker may have noted the listener's disapproving reaction and is escaping any further judgment. He or she also may be withholding information in an effort to coerce the helper into believing he or she is an innocent victim and in need of sympathy or active help.

Some silence is filled with meaningful nonverbal communication, such as deep thought, anger, fear, or grief (such as during a wake). In such times the listener's silence permits the person to experience that which is needful for his situation at that particular time. "Being with" a person at such a time is more valuable than verbiage. Indeed, words can become irrelevant and irreverent.

EMPATHY

When communicating most completely, we are in empathy with the person. Empathy is the ability to experience the other's emotional communication from his or her point of view while also maintaining one's own intellectual and emotional perspective. In listening to another's hurt, we are seeking to understand the meaning of the message to the person. A seminary counseling professor often said to his students, "When you listen to someone's problem, it isn't necessarily the way it is. It is the way the person sees the problem!" That is the first thing we try to do when we listen to another: understand how this person is experiencing the problem. Jesus must have had in mind this total empathic communication consisting of words and nonverbal symbols and silence when he said, "He who has ears, let him hear."

PRINCIPLES OF REDEMPTIVE LISTENING

Redemptive listening focuses upon what seems to have the most meaning and significance to the person speaking. In contrast, passive listening allows the person to stumble through one's inner emotional and mental jungle without helping him or her sort out emotions or thoughts or move toward making behavior changes. These three benefits (understanding feelings, sorting out thoughts, and acting responsibly to improve the situation) are some of the desired results of redemptive listening.

The first principle of redemptive listening is to *concentrate upon the speaker,* not on oneself. This can be difficult. Often the speaker will arouse similar feelings in the listener. It is easy for the listener to respond to his or her own feelings instead of the speaker's and be unaware that this has happened. For example, someone may say, "I'm going to die." Fear of one's own death arises, and the listener says, "Now, none of that kind of talk."

Until it becomes natural, the lay shepherd should consciously remind himself or herself to listen to the words and the nonverbal symbols listed above. Listening with the "inner ear" turned to one's own feelings helps the "physical ears" to hear the other person more clearly.

Find out as soon as possible the *chief complaint.* Where is the speaker hurting the most? Sometimes this is difficult because the problem may be posed as a biblical question, such as "God and the problem of evil," while the actual problem is, "Why is God punishing me?" Or the problem may not be "teenagers today," but the speaker's teenager. When a problem is too threatening to approach directly, it may be most helpful to be patient and assist the person to ease gently into sharing it.

Reflect to the person what you hear him or her saying and feeling. Such tentative phrases as "Do I hear you saying . . . ?" and "Did I understand . . . ?"—undogmatic responses—can give the person a chance to correct your failure to hear or tell the person that he or she is not communicating his or her real message. Or it may give the person a chance to wiggle out of a corner and back away from a touchy or painful subject.

The listener's *responses should be to those messages which seem to be most significant and meaningful to the speaker.* This will assist the person to utilize the time to the best advantage. Occasionally check your perception by asking if you are hearing correctly. This listening task is not an easy one. But the technique in the previous point will be helpful in this endeavor.

One exception to this rule is with the very depressed person. Sometimes verbalizing deepens the depression. In this case, the helping procedure could be to point out what is happening and to direct the person's thinking in terms of listing resources and personal strengths that might be of help. Or ask the person to list possible solutions and evaluate their consequences. Depression-lifting and emotion-calming activities seek to change the person's focus from feeling to constructive problem solving and action.

Ask for clarification or details if you are unable to follow the torrent of confused words and feelings. This is important not only if the lay shepherd is to understand the person, but it is also saying to the person that you, the listener, are interested and are trying to understand.

Occasionally summarize the message. This serves the purpose of bringing order to the conversation and stimulates the speaker to develop more fully his or her thinking on the problem. It may also help stop repetition of themes.

In a situation involving more than one contact, it may be helpful to *determine with the patient the goals of the redemptive listening relationship.* Sometimes the goal might be to examine a problem in all its facets. Helping the person examine a problem's components, securing information, pointing to how his or her emotions are influencing intellectual processes, and encouraging the person to act responsibly are all possible goals. Or the goal may be to refer the person to a professional counselor or physician, etc. It is important that both parties know the goals being pursued.

Sometimes a person needs an *emotional catharsis.* Responses to feelings, especially negative ones, asking, "How did you feel when . . . ?" and calling attention to contradictions (which indicate inner conflicts), assist in the free flow of feelings. Be careful at this point; it is easy to overencourage, especially if the person is highly emotional by nature.

Resist the temptation of curiosity. Do not probe into the nature or origin of the illness or accident for the "juicy" sinful information. If the person wants to share this information, fine; but let the initiation rest with the person. Curiosity is one's own self-interest seeking information. The listener's own needs have become the object being pursued.

A doctor does not use every medicine on one person; neither will a lay shepherd use all these principles in one visit. Those used will be the ones appropriate to the person's need. But over a period of time all of them will prove helpful to the person needing a redemptive listening ministry that develops wholeness.

BARRIERS TO LISTENING

Few listening opportunities for lay shepherds will be by appointment with the confidentiality of an office and the protection of the time given for the appointment. The medical model from the psychiatric profession is not the best one for the lay person or clergy. Most helping contacts after discharge will be in homes, at coffee breaks, between appointments, while entertaining, etc. It is well to recognize the barriers to listening, to minimize their damage, and to use them whenever possible.

Consider language itself. The word "language" in my desk dictionary has six definitions. In addition, all of us have our own private definitions for some words. And some feelings, religious experiences, and philosophical concepts do not have words adequate to express them. As one man said to me, "If I can find a word larger than 'thank you,' I'll use it; until then, thank you." How *does* one express great gratitude? Add to the inadequacy of language itself the limited ability we all have in using the language. There are very few poets and novelists.

Consider also that the listener may be preoccupied with another matter. Some people are like the person who said she had a "one-track mind." In that case, it is not possible to take on another's problem. It is best to excuse oneself from a conversation and offer a time later in the day or week. Such attention to a future meeting time indicates interest and probably will not be interpreted by the person as a rebuff.

We must also list impatience in the listener. This may be brought about by the speaker's many words and insignificant (to his listener) meanings, or the speaker may be hesitant or unable to express himself or herself. He or she may be under heavy sedation, influenced by the side effects of medication, or under the influence of a disease process.

Closely related to impatience is a condemning, judgmental spirit in the listener. Not only will this create impatience in the listener who "just can't stand him being that way," but it also may silence the person who can't tolerate any more condemnation. It must also be pointed out that some people wish to be judged and receive a neurotic enjoyment from it. But taking a pound of flesh for an ounce of sin is not redemption and is contrary to the purposes of redemptive listening.

Arguing is a barrier. It surfaces as many games. Arguing may be one-upmanship or self-justification. It may be personality rigidity that refuses to permit another to hold a different opinion. Other games could be mentioned, but the end result of all is alienation.

For the lay person, perhaps the biggest barriers are distractions, interruptions, and lack of privacy. These cannot always be guarded against but can be recognized, and it can be mutually agreed that conversation can be resumed later at a better location. In the hospital, treatments and other visitors will probably be the greatest distractions to lengthy redemptive visits.

A discussion of barriers to listening can go on and on. Some others we list in closing are: fear of being changed, fear of close relationships, the listener's fear of silence, shock in the listener at what has been said, and premature and dogmatic giving of advice. Barriers are inevitable. Our attitude toward them is not to curse the darkness but to accept them and overcome them if possible. Our goal is too high to be overcome, for it is to meet the human need for more abundant living in Christ.

BEING/DOING/KNOWING

"Tell me what to do." "I don't know what to say!" "I feel so awkward when I know someone is going to die." These statements should be read as having such mixed emotions accompanying the words as desperation, fear (of doing harm), helplessness, etc. It is a valid need to ask for and to master the "how to." To be able to *respond* appropriately, to *guide,* and to *intervene* redemptively are part of shepherding. But it has a danger. Counseling tools can become "techniquish." Methods can crowd out the "being" components in the relationship. This danger can take the form of depression in the freshman helper when he or she reads the above nine helping acts and then compares them to his or her present knowledge and performance.

Indeed, this danger leads into a larger discussion of the roles of being, doing, and knowing in affecting growth. I subscribe to the primacy of being. Knowing and doing derive from being. The lesson was dramatically demonstrated to me by a psychiatrist during my chaplaincy internship. I asked him how he explained the healing and growth that took place in his patients. He responded, "I live with someone for an hour a week and let the Holy Spirit do what he will."

Ask the *helpers* what facilitates growth, and they will point you to their professional literature which says, "It is reality therapy," or "Perles's gestalt approach and dream interpretation methodology is the growing edge of psychiatry today." Others say, "No, behavior modification is best with certain problems." All these explanations focus upon methodology and beyond to the theory and the theoretician.

But ask those *helped,* and they will say, "She cared for me when no one else would." "He was *there* when I needed him." Here the emphasis is upon "being" a loving, caring person. The relationship between "knowing," "being," and "doing" cannot be treated in depth here. But the helper should be aware of these components in the helping relationship.

An excellent treatment of the subject from the biblical perspective has been given by Dr. William B. Oglesby, Jr. I recommend that the more serious student secure a copy of his paper. He states that from the biblical perspective, people are sinners who need forgiveness and reconciliation from which "comes both right knowing and right doing."[1]

Critics of the church show that *being* is primary when they comment, "Those hypocrites!" "That is a "cold" church; no one will speak to you."

Listening is more than hearing with the ear. It is entering into the inner world of another with the purpose of being with, accepting, understanding, and helping the person understand his or her own self. It results also in helping the person arrive at decisions as to what actions are needed to resolve or live with the present life situation.

7

Praying with the Sick

The mood of this age is inquisitive and skeptical: "Prove it"; "Show me." The criteria are often (subconsciously to many but more consciously to the serious student) those of the physical sciences. However, the research tools of the physical sciences are not adequate in the study of prayer. Since prayer does not lend itself to scientific medical investigation, we may quote Alfred, Lord Tennyson from his work *Morte d'Arthur:* "More things are wrought by prayer than this world dreams of." At the start, we must acknowledge our dependence upon religious experience and our lack of knowledge of the mechanics of prayer and of how much healing comes from prayer and how much from scientific medicine.* Both activities are going on simultaneously. In spite of these difficulties, there is much we can say that will make our prayers for healing more effective.

Imagine a hypothetical interview. Mr. Jones is a fifty-nine-year-old farmer. He is in the hospital for kidney surgery. In the conversation he expresses:

DOUBT—about his doctor's ability ("What do you know about my specialist?").

FEAR—He calls himself a "baby" when it comes to pain.

ANXIETY—He expresses concern over his family who are on the road to the hospital at this time ("I wonder why my family isn't here.").

VOCATIONAL UNCERTAINTY—He wonders if the surgery will keep him from putting in his crops next year ("How long does it take

---

* The specific application of this treatment of intercessory prayer is illness. However, the principles are valid for other needs.

to get over this surgery? I don't have anybody helping me any more.").

What kind of prayer would you have with this man? Would you lift up the dangers of undergoing anesthesia? Remind God that sinners go to hell (while hoping the patient will hear you!)? Perhaps some persons do, for some patients turn down an offer for prayer, with the statement, "No, it frightens me."

SOME PRINCIPLES FOR PRAYING WITH THE SICK

We begin with the faith that all prayer is addressed to God, while also the hearing of the prayer is a means of grace for us mortals. Our *primary purpose in praying for healing is to help the person relate to God.* It is not easy to fulfill this purpose. For example, it is easy for the visitor to use prayer as a way of getting out of tight situations, such as anxious conversations about death or why God permits evil to happen to good people. It is a common error to use prayer to relieve our personal anxiety while serving in the role of helper.

Nor are we preaching or teaching the patient. Some corporate prayer may have a teaching element, *but intercessory prayer's primary purpose is assisting the person* in relating to the Master Physician. This teaching purpose is valid, but it is subordinate to the primary one of relating the person to God. Prayer is a form of spiritual, interpersonal relationship. Many people appreciate Paul Tillich's theology, but his symbol of God, "Ground of Being," may be too impersonal a symbol for praying people.

Our farmer, Mr. Jones, will surely be listening to us as we pray aloud. He may even learn something, but prayer is primarily an interpersonal spiritual experience of fellowship involving God, visitor, patient, and others present.

Next, when praying, we should always *stress the presence of God rather than his gifts.* The Reverend Lewis Maclachlan tells the following story which illustrates this principle:

The pastor of a London parish received a visit from a man and woman who were desperate. The man had gotten reports from tests which indicated the presence of an incurable illness. He and his wife acknowledged that they had neglected God and made promises of better living before God. They also wanted the minister to pray for spiritual healing. An appointment was made for them to receive instruction in prayer. On the day of the appointment, the minister received a call from the man. In patronizing tones, he assured the minister that his efforts were no longer needed. The hospital had given him another person's reports in error. His condition would respond to treatment, and thus he no longer had need for prayer, church, or God.[1]

Many people are like this. They have no need for God on sunny days but only when crises occur. And even then they demonstrate that they have no need for God, only for his gifts. We might also add that these people often fail to see that God can use them. So often these are "good people," but their goodness is not put to work. They are good-for-nothing.

A minister asked my opinion on a counseling case. A woman with a thirty-year-old, unmarried, alcoholic son had been praying for his healing. Part of the son's difficulty was that his father had always rejected him and "made" him feel worthless. The woman was disturbed that her prayers for her son were unanswered. The minister responded that she was praying for the wrong thing. She should be praying for her husband's conversion. His reasoning for this was that if the father would correct his own attitude toward the son, the son would not feel the need to drink. The minister's advice, though partial and minimizing the son's responsibility for his behavior, points to a truth. We thrive on the love and faith significant people place in us. The most significant personal influence upon us is God. Faith is a relationship with God, and blessings come from it, including health. Prayer for healing seeks the presence of the Father more than his gifts. To prize a gift more than the giver is to love the creation more than the Creator.

Third, the prayer should *lift up the spiritual, emotional, social, and physical needs and strengths expressed* by our friend Mr. Jones. These needs are conscious, though you may be aware of needs which are unconscious to the person. These needs become his or her point of contact with the healing powers of God. However, prayer does not focus upon these needs. The focus is upon God and the gift of wholeness. Needs are merely symptoms. Our end is not symptomatic relief but whole healing.

Such prayers show that one's needs, fears, and sins are items which are to be shared, not denied or repressed. We are the ones who need to deny and repress in order to protect our egos and self-images. God already knows what we are like. The hardest part is in *admitting to ourselves* what we are like. When the person acknowledges to us and to God his or her unacceptable self, the person is in effect giving this self to us to give to God. Such self-honesty and acceptance of self, plus our acceptance and God's acceptance, often result in a "cleansing" feeling.

Needs expressed nonverbally through anxiety, body language,

etc., may be dealt with, but do so with caution. Bringing these unconscious needs to consciousness may further agitate the patient. This is usually a strict "no-no" before surgery. Most, if not all, people have enough fear and anxiety, and these emotions constrict blood vessels, tighten muscles, and release adrenalin, to name a few physical changes.

In confession, try using a general prayer (or Scripture) rather than asking God to forgive the person of sins for which he has not acknowledged the need for forgiveness. Often I will ask the person what he or she wants me to put in the prayer. If a request for forgiveness is made, it is included in a form considered appropriate for the occasion.

Fourth, when praying for others, *we are mediators,* and people see us this way. Make the best use of the role. As a minister I sometimes hear, "Preacher, I can't seem to get through. Will you pray for me?" But strong "church pillars" are often seen as persons whom God will hear "quicker than he will hear ordinary Christian, miserable me." It is proper that we acknowledge this role and be the sick person's intercessor. The other half, or perhaps the major portion, of our mediating function is to emphasize and be a channel for God's Holy Spirit. Some of the fruits of the Spirit as they relate to healing are faith, hope, peace, love, purpose, and patience. If we show strong belief, are at peace, and show love for the patient, he or she will pick these things up in the atmosphere. During the stress of illness, these supportive aspects of the gospel generally take priority over insight and confrontation or prophetic aspects.

One warning is in order. Regression and dependency are common emotional responses to threatening illnesses and accidents. To be asked to pray "for" someone may be an attempt to shift responsibility to the intercessor. Whether this be the situation or not, it is probably best in all cases to respond to a "pray for me," with an offer to pray "with" the person.

A mediator is assisting a relationship; therefore, the use of scare literature dealing with sin and sickness and damnation is OUT. John Wesley said, "I preach law until conviction; then I preach grace for decision." The patient is already scared and needs to experience the safety and reassurances of God's salvation which we symbolize in our loving relationship.

Dr. Leslie Weatherhead, quoting a shepherd, says that in times of danger the sheep look to the shepherd, not to the source of danger.[2] In times of illness, we tend to concentrate on our pain and problems. Like the sheep, we, too, need to look to our source of help, God, and those he has called to heal us. Faith healers say they concentrate not on the illness but upon Christ or God, his resources and character; or sometimes they entertain a mental image of the person as he or she would be if whole.

A fifth principle is that prayer should, in general, *be positive.* One way to achieve this is to support the ill person's faith and strengths. The Bible records several ways in which this is done.

1. In the Psalms, past victories are recalled. Spiritual strength in the recall seems to take the form of awakening expectancy of help and hope for recovery in the present crisis. (See Psalms 42:4-5; 44-1; 116.)
2. The prayer might also recall to the person problem-solving techniques that worked before and can be expected to work now. One such way is seen in the psalmist's calling for help from friends and temple worshipers. Some people resort to pills for purposes of escape. Others reach out for people. The Bible recommends the latter approach. (This does not rule out medication being used in responsible ways by doctors.)
3. Help the patient remember that he or she has a strong faith (if this is true). The patient is not a jellyfish. Through the years, God has built his or her Christian character. Thank God for this steadfastness as John does of the churches of Revelation.

Prayers of thanksgiving and affirmation fall in the category of "positive." It is good to experience, to affirm, and to express the gratitude, joy, faith, hope, love, etc., which we feel. The principle is true here: "What we do not use, we lose."

Sixth, prayer with the sick should also *acknowledge the reality of the many ways God heals:* through faith, through "talking therapy" or counseling, through scientific medicine's medication, radiation, surgery, or physical manipulation. On one occasion, the disciples wanted a man to stop healing in Jesus' name. Likewise, we, too, tend to restrict the ways we will recognize God's healing activity.

It is appropriate and necessary that we pray for those who are God's human healing servants. Doctors and paramedical specialists are utilizing God's laws of healing. They are mediators. They are also human and have hang-ups and grow weary and discouraged. We should acknowledge their efforts and pray for them.

Seventh, *sometimes the person must be prepared for the prayer.* This can be done in three ways:

1. By offering emotional release—this may be facilitated by

offering an opportunity to talk or cry.

2. By determining needs—ask, "What would you like for me to put in this prayer?"
3. By testing his or her faith in prayer's ability to mediate God's healing power—ask, "How do you feel about prayer as a resource in helping you?" or "What do you feel about prayer in a situation such as yours?"

Eighth, prayer must *be honest.* Jesus' prayer in the garden of Gethsemane is an example of honest praying. Honesty in prayer can be very difficult. But it is more helpful to pray, "I'm afraid of dying," than to pray, "Thy will be done," when we don't want his will and are angry about it. This honest prayer allows the expression of fears and anger within the context of God's accepting love. Honest prayer paves the way for sincerely asking for God's presence and willingly sharing in whatever comes to pass. Thus, if healing is denied, we are assured that we are not alone and are sustained by his spiritual presence.

The last point is that too much religion is "word without action." We must *respond to prayer with commitment.* Jesus often told people to do some witnessing or service after he had healed them. In doing this, he changed their style of life which might have contributed to the illness. He also has given them a purpose for living. Too often in counseling a person, no corrective action or alternative behavior is expected and done, and the counseling is not effective. We must *respond to prayer* with action.

These are my reflections on healing prayers in general. There are times when special techniques may be called for or special considerations taken. For example, with the acute stroke patient in the early stages of illness or with the patient in a stupor, try utilizing the language and simplicity of childhood religion with its trusting, loving relationship with Jesus. Or use prayers from Scriptures or prayers familiar to the patient. And always speak slowly and distinctly.

One day my young son asked a question about lightning. We turned to the encyclopedia for the answer. In reading the article, we discovered that as the bolt of lightning approaches the ground or a tall object in contact with the ground, a small electrical charge about one hundred feet long, called a "leader," jumps from the ground. This small charge of electricity creates the final pathway of the bolt of lightning. When healing comes through prayer, prayer can be thought of as the small power from us that releases the tremendous healing power of God.

8

Personal Lay Pastoral Evangelism

A head nurse asked me to see a patient who had been upset by a minister. After introducing myself to the patient and explaining the purpose of my visit, he told me that a part-time minister, Bible in hand, had come into his room. The clergyman said, "Mr. S——, I'm Reverend B——. Your second cousin J——told me you were bad sick and not active in a church. He asked me to come by and pray for your soul. Are you saved, Mr. S——?" The patient responded with, "My soul is none of your d—— business! See that door? Git out of it as fast as you got in it." This was followed by three hours of elevated blood pressure reading in the patient.

A patient in the intensive care unit wrote a letter to me upon his discharge. I quote a portion: "A minister visited me at a time that I was struggling for my life. He first asked if I was saved, then proceeded to pray as if I would surely die." Fortunately, such insensitive clerical visits are rare. Unfortunately, ones like these are remembered by the doctor and hospital staff, while thousands of helpful visits are treated with routine lack of notice.

This chapter offers some "no-no's" and "please-do's" and their "why's." The starting point is an evangelistic theology and methodology which can be called personal pastoral evangelism. This evangelism is one-to-one, in contrast to evangelism directed to large numbers of individuals personally unknown to the evangelist. It is aware of timing and multiple approaches. A helpful analogy would be that of a farmer who prepares the soil, sows, cultivates, and harvests. This evangelism is patient, supportive, and exercises discipline lovingly. It is concerned with continuing nurture. It is also personal in that it approaches people with its offer of Christ's fellowship and help at the point of their needs and strengths as well as their sins.

SOME "PLEASE-DO'S"

Chapter 2 presented the dynamics of crisis. *Please use this knowledge, and relate the grace of God to the crisis needs and opportunities.* Faith has proved helpful in successful outcomes of healing experiments. Faith, hope, and love are intangibles with healing properties.[1] The use of prayer, the Bible, and the church supportive community was shown in chapter 2. The need to respond to and trust God is never so great as in times of crisis. And prayer is the best devotional practice for creating this attitude of responsiveness and trust.

Remember that a person in crisis is more susceptible to influence by others than he or she is during periods of stable functioning. "When the forces are, as it were, teetering in the balance, a relatively minor intervention may weigh them down to one side or the other."[2] The lay shepherd is present to assist in bringing victory. The crisis is God's opportunity.

Repeatedly I hear hospitalized persons say, "I've had lots of time to think." Their pain and need have created a "life review." They are open to new ideas and problem-solving techniques which may work better than the old ones.

A principle to employ with a person in crisis would be to explore with him or her the need and to look with the person at the ways Christ speaks to that need. The statement "Christ is the answer" is true, but Christ is the answer to what? The cliché is meaningless as long as it is generalized. It is potent when particularized!

The second "please-do" is: *Please recognize a variety of evangelistic approaches.* Much evangelism is addressed to the "sinful soul." No doubt this is a needful approach, but this approach is not the only one. In John 1:35-51 we see Jesus making his appeal to the (1) needs and (2) strengths of those whom he called to be apostles. Andrew and the beloved disciple came with two needs. One was centered in the Law and expressed itself in their addressing Jesus as Rabbi, or "teacher" of the Law. The second need involved their hope: the coming of the Messiah. Jesus met them at their belief and hope needs; he taught them the fulfillment of the Law in himself and of the hoped-for Messiah who had come.

Jesus offered Peter personality fulfillment. He, in Jesus' fellowship, would not always be a weak ego, but would develop into a "rock," a character who would testify to God's power to change and mature a person.

Nathaniel, in contrast, had a developed character ready to be used. "Behold an Israelite indeed, in whom is no guile!" (John 1:47). Probably he was a serious student of the Old Testament because the shade of the fig tree was considered the proper place for studying the Scriptures (John 1:48).

Philip, like Andrew, was a man of action. Both men had to share that which excited them. Jesus needs people who are willing to share their convictions with friends and family.

The list of persons transformed by Jesus and the variety of approaches extend beyond the original twelve apostles. Paul was a trained theologian and a Pharisee. God converted him and used his many talents. Jesus met a woman, caught in adultery, at her moral need. And Nicodemus was ministered to at his need for spiritual rebirth (John 3:1-21).

> Yet upon each one is placed the necessity for a mature, manly choice: "Whom do *you* say I am?" The answer must always be the same: "The Christ of God" (Luke 9:20), but the way in which a man finds that answer will be his own. In the process of new birth, the Spirit of God is as free as the wind (John 3:8).[3]

A third "please-do" is: *Please select carefully your motivating tools.* The damaging consequences of guilt and fear are dealt with later in the chapter. But a positive treatment may be helpful at this point. A chaplain supervisor asked his interns if they knew the difference between a preacher and pastor. Sensing this as a rhetorical question, they replied in the negative. The supervisor explained, "A preacher gleefully says, 'You are going to hell, and I'm enjoying every step you take.' A pastor says, 'You are going to hell, and each step you take breaks both God's heart and mine.'" The message is the same in both cases—"You are going to hell"—but the motivating spirit is not. Jesus wept over Jerusalem. Exercise a loving spirit to others and a thankful spirit to God. Many people who are in crisis feel enough guilt already. The person may be under conviction as a result of his "life-review reflections." If the sense of conviction is there, then love will reap the harvest. Judgment will be as the hot sun burning up the tender plant of repentance.

Are you grateful for the blessing of your life in Christ? How can you keep it under a bushel? Do you rejoice in the blessings of God as did the writer of Psalm 16? The person in crisis will "pick up" this loving/grateful spirit in you, and both of you will be blessed.

Another "please-do" is: *Please use time and timing.* The farmer prepares the soil, plants, cultivates, and harvests. Too many Christians are on a "harvest hang-up." They will not or do not know how to plant and cultivate. We do well to heed Paul's words: "I planted, Apollos watered, but God gave the growth" (1 Corinthians 3:6).

The end result of personal pastoral evangelism may be emotional/spiritual: gratitude, joy, zeal in witness, excitement, peace, love, etc. But it is more. It is also redemptive action and witness. Paul speaks of fruits and gifts of the Holy Spirit. The Sermon on the Mount is a composite picture of the life in Christ created in the Christian by the Holy Spirit.

To be more specific: The demoniac was clothed and in his right mind and witnessing to the love of God. Zacchaeus made restitution for his tax-collecting sins (Luke 19:1-10). The jailer at Philippi shared the Good News with his family and, as was the custom, directed that they take his new faith and be baptized (Acts 16:33). Joseph of Arimathea gave his tomb to Jesus. A leper came back to thank Jesus for his cure.

A healthy body and mind are important. But a person may be "good-for-nothing," that is, he or she may serve no cause or mission outside the needs of his or her immediate family. Persons need God-given action goals through which to express their newfound God consciousness.

SOME "NO-NO'S"

Anything in this world, it seems, can be misused, and this includes evangelism. Here are some ways evangelism can be counterproductive.

Do not use fear and guilt to motivate someone in a crisis. This is especially true for a physically ill person. These emotions create changes in hormone and body chemistry. Slight changes applied to already chemically unbalanced bodies may result in a worsening of the patient's physical condition. The body has a self-preservation mechanism which responds to threat.* This mechanism is called the "fight or flight" syndrome. The consciously experienced emotion of fear stimulates the pituitary gland to release the hormone ACTH. ACTH goes to the adrenal glands which produce the hormones epinephrine, norepinephrine, and catecholamine. Epinephrine or adrenalin (which is the same hormone) increases the body metabolism and blood sugar. It has a tendency to slow down the

---

* I am indebted to Dr. Robert Carter, M.D., for checking physiological details of this self-preservation discussion.

bowel activities and also stimulates the kidney to constrict the output of urine. Norepinephrine, which is released by the adrenal glands, has two functions. One is to stimulate the heart to increase its rate. At the same time it also constricts or closes down slightly the blood vessels in the arms and legs. If the patient has a coronary artery which is partially clogged with atherosclerosis, this increased heart rate could precipitate angina, an excruciating chest pain which results when the heart is not receiving enough blood for its own nourishment. The constriction of the coronary arteries may well result in a complete occlusion (closing), thus resulting in a myocardial infarction (heart attack). The catecholamines (adrenal carticosteriods) which are released by the adrenal glands have multiple functions, such as increasing the acid content of the body and retaining fluid.

Assume a sixty-five-year-old man has coronary artery disease with approximately 70 percent occlusion. Place him in a fearful situation which results in an increased cardiac rate as well as constriction of the coronary vessels down to 90 percent. This patient might well develop a myocardial infarction. The myocardial infarction (heart attack) that results is thus due to the fact that an adequate blood supply is not getting to that particular portion of the heart.

Guilt and depression also stimulate the pituitary gland through the hypothalamus with similar results. The chronic ACTH level in a depressed or anxious person is elevated but not to the same extreme as that of the person who is placed in a "fight or flight" syndrome.

People with long-term anxieties (stress jobs, for example) quite often develop a chronic tachycardia (increased heart rate). This increased heart rate, along with atherosclerosis, can develop into hypertension. The outcome of this sequence could be a stroke. Books have been written on the effects of stress and emotions on the body organ systems. We only add here that chronic anger contributes to stomach ulcer formation, and fear and anxiety are harmful to the diabetic.

In conclusion, if you use guilt and fear to motivate a person to "receive Christ" and if you add the demand that he make an instant decision which increases his anxiety, you may shorten his life on earth. If he isn't able, because of his physical condition, to "get right" with God, your evangelistic technique may create the opposite result.

It is also a "no-no" to treat a person as a thing or a partial being. The above mentioned part-time minister's concern with the patient's "soul" is not Jesus' approach. He was concerned with the "whole person": "Are ye angry at me, because I have made a man every whit whole on the sabbath day?" (John 7:23, KJV). We saw the scope of his ministry in chapter 1. We do not like being treated impersonally and called by number. (Social Security or room number) nor being referred to as "that kidney in room 666." Nor do we respond to being thought of as a disembodied soul when we know we are total beings loved by God and loving God with "all your heart, and with all your soul, and with all your strength, and with all your mind" (Luke 10:27).

"Instant evangelism"[4] is a term used by Dr. Samuel Southard to describe a current popular form of evangelism which stresses an urgent, immediate response from a person to give his or her soul to Christ. Guilt and fear, "hellfire and damnation," are commonly used to motivate. Such evangelism initially was historically limited (associated with American revivalism) and culturally localized (conservative Protestantism, mainly among middle and poor classes). This evangelistic theology and methodology obviously have an appeal to many. Some people, without doubt, need a strong, urgent message about the quality of their lives. But when, without thought to consequences, instant evangelism's strong and weak points are carried over for use with those in crises, the results create such a large percentage of destructive reactions that they, to use a medical term, make its use "contraindicative," that is, a "no-no"!

Organized hospital evangelism is also a "no-no." Occasionally church groups develop a "mission" to convert the sick, assuming that all in the hospital are lost souls in need of salvation. Such an approach fails to respect each person as an individual. It assumes that this particular evangelistic approach is good for all cases and occasions. It views the patient as a stereotyped "sinner" being punished by God with sickness. Equating sickness and sin is a simplistic explanation of the very complex relationship between sin and sickness.

Having given the above "no-nos" in evangelistic work with those in crisis, do not go to the other extreme of neglecting the need for spiritual correction when it is indicated, when no damage is seen to the person as a complicating factor. In Matthew we have instructions for disciplining church members (Matthew 18:15-22). Paul instructs us to "admonish the idlers, encourage the fainthearted . . ." (1 Thessalonians 5:14; see also Titus 2:1-10).

At this point one "please-do" should be inserted. How does one exercise spiritual correction? First, do not push, try to convict, convince of error, or argue. Some problems are such that if approached "head on," all persons come away with a headache.

Instead, an *invitation* to discuss the quality of religious life might be given, such as "I've noticed that many people engage in a 'life review' when ill a long time. How about you?" A Baptist minister friend and I were having coffee with some of his laymen. One man was angry and told how he was going to "teach a lesson" to a person who had wronged him. His minister said quietly but firmly, "You don't want to do that." "Why not?" asked the surprised man. The minister quietly explained the dangerous consequences that would follow "the lesson." This minister did not present himself as the law and gospel incarnate but appealed to the parishioner's common sense and good moral sense. In this way, if the parishioner wanted to argue, it would be with himself, Jesus, the Ten Commandments, the Bible, etc., and not the minister.

When dealing with a moral or disciplinary issue, "please do" note the person's emotions and the body's symptoms of distress. If the discussion is upsetting, back away and deal with it later. The topic has been introduced, reflection upon it has begun, and we may patiently let the Holy Spirit do any necessary convicting and redeeming. Resist the pride that would bid you persist so you can have a bragging testimony of what God has done (through you, of course, as his mighty spiritual servant).

When engaged in spiritual correction, be careful—as careful as a skillful surgeon with his scalpel. He hurts in order to heal, but he is careful to hurt no more than is necessary.

9

The Church's Supportive Ministry

Think back over your life to a time when you had "problems" which would not "go away." How were you supported by your family, friends, and church? Many answers could be given to this question:

"A man makes it fine until mealtime. Then he never forgets that unexpected hot dish brought in for him and the children to eat."

"I had many problems. I was hit by the second one while still reeling from the first. My friend came and sensed my feelings. He sat beside me and gave me time just to be silent."

"She was the kind of person who saw needs. And when it was obvious no one was going to meet them, she said she was going to do them."

"Let's don't forget the military. They stick together."

"After my husband died, Bill, a neighbor, would take my boys with his to the ball games."

"My pastor was there when I needed him. I remember one time he just put his hand on my shoulder and let me cry."

"My physician helped me alleviate my guilt. He was so understanding. Anytime I called he would let me talk."

The root meaning of "support," according to Funk and Wagnall's Standard College Dictionary, is *sup* (a variation of *sub*, meaning "up from under") plus *potare* ("to carry"). The definition of the adjective *supportive* is "providing support." Thus, a "supportive ministry" is a relationship in which we help someone "get under" a problem the person must carry himself or herself. You will note that this definition stresses the responsibility of the person being helped to carry his or her own load. A major problem in supportive ministry is overdependency, in which the load is placed by the person on the helper. This must be avoided.

Suppose a problem or crisis cannot return a person to a prior, superior life. What then? Some people make no decision or do not accept the imposed changes, unrealistically fighting their fate. They fail to see their new limits and fail to realize the possibilities open to them. Overcome by hopelessness and depression, they become candidates for additional failure. The crisis has come to stay and to produce additional "demons" to torment the person and family. In supportive counseling, it is assumed that no major change in health or life-style will occur immediately and, therefore, the aim is to support the patient in his or her present circumstances.

Dr. Howard Clinebell says, "In supportive counseling the pastor uses those counseling methods which *stabilize, undergird, nurture, motivate or guide* troubled persons, enabling them to handle their problems and relationships more constructively. . . ."[1] We can use this statement as a goal statement. Again, the relationship is a *helping* one, and the person is responsible for his or her own decisions and responses.

"Increasing ego strength" is a nebulous expression and is considered here as a goal. Clinebell quotes Eric Erikson's components of a strong ego: "Virtues such as hope, purpose, competence, fidelity, love, care, and wisdom are vital elements in the ego's strength."[2] We hope that the end process will be sustaining and even beyond to "weller than well," a term used by Dr. Karl Menninger to indicate a person who has moved through a crisis and has learned how to handle emotions and problems better.

A unique contribution of the church to wholeness has been clearly suggested by Dr. John B. Cobb, Jr. He relates the sexual problems of a parishioner, Chester, and the efforts of Pastor Jones to help. While the psychiatrist is helping Chester with the removal of this particular problem, the church can fill the meaning and value vacuum in Chester's life.

He can be related to groups in the church that are engaged in service of others as well as mutual help. It may be that involvement with others in such service can create healthy relations with his peers just as effectively as therapy. Perhaps the sexual preoccupations can be lessened as other things take on greater importance in his life.[3]

This tentatively worded statement of Dr. Cobb is in harmony with Jesus' actions in giving the demoniac a mission to perform in the kingdom of God (Mark 5:19-20). It is in harmony with Jesus' parable of the man who cleared his house of a demon, and because he left it empty, seven demons worse than the first came to live in it. This type of ministry is growth oriented and supportive. It is to be found only in a community that lives together in the spirit of Christ, forgiving, renewing, giving, sharing.

The discussion thus far has emphasized the Second Great Commandment (Matthew 22:34-40)—what we good Samaritans do to love our ill or troubled neighbor. But it should not be forgotten that this is not a purely humanistic concern. The Second Commandment of service to neighbor is in the context of the First Commandment—to love God. This first relationship provides the direction, motivation, and healing power for the proper fulfillment of the second.

SPECIAL APPLICATION TO LONG-TERM HOSPITALIZATION

"I'm so tired of all this! "I'm weary, bone weary." "I did not realize how you can lose so much strength being in bed this long." These statements were made by "nice" patients who have accepted and made a fairly good adjustment to long-term hospitalization.

Some patients are not "nice." They complain, fight the staff, talk of lawsuits, refuse medicines, and a small number go home without medical approval. A common syndrome is when "patience goes home before the patient." Sometimes we see "giving-up-itis." Dr. George L. Engel describes a "giving-up—given-up complex" which precedes the onset of illness. The clinical manifestations are also seen in those hospitalized a long time and in those in nursing homes. Dr. Engel gives the following characteristics:

(1) the giving-up affects of helplessness or hopelessness; (2) a depreciated image of oneself; (3) a loss of gratification from relationships or roles in life; (4) a disruption of the sense of continuity between past, present, and future; (5) a reactivation of memories of earlier and periods of giving-up.[4]

In this special situation, supportive counseling may be supplemented with hope therapy. This ministry can be emotionally draining, for in my experience, it seems at times that these people actually draw emotional energy out of the helper.

SUPPORT MINISTRY COMPONENTS

We respond immediately to help a person in crisis. But what if the crisis is not resolved, and the patient's life stays at a new level requiring continuing efforts to prevent further deterioration? There is need at this point for a support ministry.

An effective support ministry has many components. It may include a "hospital closet." These are hospital room furnishings and other medical supplies, such as hospital beds, walkers, crutches, bedpans, over-the-bed tables, etc. They are "checked out" for use and returned when the need is over or after a specified time.

The support ministry must be well staffed with "talent banks" of church members and their times of availability. Especially helpful for this lay shepherding ministry are persons already professionally involved in helping people. These include vocational and school counselors and social workers. Christian doctors, especially psychiatrists and clinical psychologists, could offer consultation services as part of their "offering" or "witness" to the power of the healing Christ. The philosophical vacuum of humanism and the secular context of much government-sponsored ministry is stifling to many Christians.

Funding, both administrative and emergency, is necessary. Many pastors are provided with emergency discretionary funds.

The active leadership of the pastor and the church's administrative board is essential.*

Timing and the use of time are frequently overlooked as elements in the helping relationship. Time is perceived as a relative matter. It "stands still." The older we are, the faster it "flies." Someone has said that a sermon "need not be eternal to be immortal." A boring lecture is lengthy, while a stimulating, relevant one is "over" before the lecturer got started.

"You'll get over it and find someone else to marry"—not only was this a crude statement, but also it was said only two days after the wife's husband had packed his things and moved in with another woman. Sometimes the right answer can be given at the wrong time: "You are not going to be part of the wreckage." This may be necessary as a "shock" statement to someone in chronic depression. It is inappropriate if said in the emergency room when the husband realizes he will live but that his wife died in the automobile accident. He doesn't believe, at that moment, that he will not yet be part of the wreckage. The appropriate time is when the person in the chronic condition says to himself or herself, "I realized others had been through what I was going through. They were not part of the wreckage, and I need not be either." This person was in the ending

* Both this point and the one preceding it are discussed in the next chapter.

stage of grief. For her, this was fourteen months after her teenager's death.

Time and timing are related to many factors; its redemptive use is probably more a matter of intuition than scientific skill and knowledge. Timing is very important. Never forget it as a key component in supportive counseling.

PREVENTION OF ILLNESS THROUGH SUPPORTIVE MINISTRY

The Judeo-Christian heritage coming through the church offers thousands of years of experience in different social contexts with their different needs. The church's supportive ministry can be a significant factor in the drive to keep health costs from rising faster than other segments of our national economy. Our efforts should also increase health.

Our contribution can be in the prevention of illness. Most Old Testament dietary and sanitary laws served (and still serve) the need for prevention of illness. Leprosy in the Old Testament was a term used to describe many diseases of the skin. Regulations (laws) to contain the spread of these illnesses have been called the "first models of sanitary legislation." When leprosy spread through Europe in the thirteenth and fourteenth centuries, the physicians were overwhelmed by the magnitude of the epidemic. When they failed to contain the illness, the church addressed the problem by applying the laws of Leviticus 13, and the epidemic was contained. The application of biblical sanitation measures has no doubt been effective on many other occasions with other illnesses. Indeed, many of today's sanitary and illness-prevention measures can be shown to be similar to the principles upon which Mosaic laws are based.

What were they? Moses' law included washing the body and clothes in running water (a shower is cleaner than a bath). He instructed that the upper lip be covered (face mask to prevent the spread of airborne germs?). Banishment from the community (isolation?) and the burning or washing of contaminated clothing (secondary infection controls?) were also part of the instructions. An unclean condition lasted until sundown (to give the sun's ultraviolet rays adequate time to complete their work of sterilization?). Another rule involved inspection of the ill person by a priest (health officer for the community?). Add to the above measures the laws (health regulations) applied to persons who handled corpses. These laws included the washing or breaking of uncovered cooking pots and washing the body during seven days of uncleanliness (isolation? See

Numbers 19:11-22). Also, certain unclean "swarming creatures" are listed. The mouse is among them. If a mouse got in a pot of food, the food was thrown away, and the pot was washed or broken (Leviticus 11:29-38). The sanitary disposal of human excrement is found in Deuteronomy 23:12-13. The remedy is so simple—bury it.

Many of the biblical reasons given for these health matters are ceremonial. The ancient Hebrew probably knew nothing of cholesterol and germs. The interesting thing is that the instructions still stand, though today we have discovered through scientific research different reasons to honor them. Old Testament dietary and sanitary laws served (and still serve) the need for prevention of illness. In those ancient times, when you became ill, you faced the prospect of limited means of cure. It was essential that you not get sick. This is true even today. It is better not to have a stroke or heart attack or diabetes. Today, healing is an advanced art, but the cost has become so great that who can afford to get sick? Prevention is part of the religious heritage that is assuming increased importance today, for the old and for a new reason. God wants us to have abundant life. That life includes health and freedom from unnecessary suffering. Both prevention and healing are blessings from the "LORD, your healer" (Exodus 15:26).

The church cannot tell the health care industry to do more in the matter of prevention. But the nation's health care industry can use this prevention experience and decide what part of its resources can be devoted to it and its priority in the total ministry of health care. Should the nation's health care industry decide that this is important, it would find the local churches a ready-made institution, theologically aware, eager (we hope), and with education facilities available to cooperate in offering "prevention of illness" as one answer to health care costs. But more important for the church is that in this cooperative endeavor it is carrying out the mission of Christ who went about preaching, teaching, and healing.

Paul Tournier has summarized the wholeness of our approach and the relationship of healing and support:

> It has been said of medicine that its duty is sometimes to heal, often to afford relief, and always to bring consolation. This is exactly what the Bible tells us that God does for suffering humanity. Sometimes God heals, but not always [2 Corinthians 12:9]. But He gives relief, He protects and sustains us in times of affliction; and His consolation is unending. Here too we may say that the doctor in his vocation works hand in hand with God.[5]

10

The Care and Feeding of Lay Shepherding Groups:
A Closing Word to Pastors and Lay Shepherds

Shepherding ministry may assume many organizational forms. The one proposed in this book (and the one to be given priority treatment in this chapter) is an officially designated group working under the direct supervision of the pastor. Other forms include: (1) an officially selected group, such as the deacons, with pastoral responsibility to certain families; (2) groups in a geographical proximity led by a "circuit rider" (lay pastor) who has been selected by the pastor or a nominating committee to assume shepherding duties for his or her church neighbors; (3) a group of Sunday school teachers, "hospital and shut-in" officers, or altar guild members who deliver flowers, etc., and who come together occasionally to exchange visitation experiences and receive training.

CHARACTERISTICS OF A SUCCESSFUL VISITATION PROGRAM

A Pastor Committed to Lay Shepherding—The pastor's commitment should be reflected in his own ministerial priorities. He should have a pastoral spirit and a strong visitation ministry. He will set aside time to deal with organizational problems and train or see that consultants are available to train the visitors. He will supervise the visitors by making assignments and will offer personal consultation to his lay shepherds.

Knowing his congregation, he can match the need with the appropriate visitor. One lay shepherd was told, "If I'm sick, I don't want a stranger from the church visiting me." The pastor would be in the best position to know this attitude and to honor it by not assigning a visitor at all. The purpose of lay visitation is not to increase the number of hospital visitors! Service is measured as quality, not quantity. The visiting pastor who knows his congregation will also know who is too ill for a visit, and thus he serves an important screening function. Some church members are blessed with family and deep friendships. Others are isolated, lonely, perhaps new to the church, and would need this ministry more than the former group would.

The pastor should have organizational skills. A newly organized visitation group will have start-up problems unique to its own situation. Enthusiasm in the visitors is usually not enough momentum to keep a group going. Assignments and visitor's schedules often fit like square pegs in round holes, and lack of communication can create problems. The attitude of the pastor toward the visiting laity is very important, especially the pastor's acceptance of the laity and the limitations of their role as well as the pastor's own sense of adequacy.[1]

The visitation group is a new thing and may be met with resistance. An occasional church member will be hostile; others will be open and will welcome help. Some, perhaps the majority, will "wait and see." I hope that this chapter will help groups move through the initial organization phase more rapidly than the groups I taught. The group needs the authority and commitment of the pastor to help meet these problems.

The pastor's leadership style should be that of coach–player or "consultation" style. This latter term, used by Wayne Oates, is compared to ". . . pilot training in flying. The consultation style calls for soloing and maintaining good radio contact at the same time."[2] The pastor trains his visitors or, from his professional education and experience, knows what needs to be taught and who the consultants are who can meet the particular training needs.

The pastor working out of his professional stance has much to offer a lay visitation program. Dr. Paul Pruyser, in his book *The Minister as Diagnostician,* points out several unique professional resources of the ordained ministry:

> awareness of the holy; understandings about Providence; faith as an objective and historical pattern of tenets; grace or gratefulness; repentance or repenting–change; communion–two or three gathered; and a sense of vocation.[3]

The coach–player leadership style may also include a "triangle" helping approach.

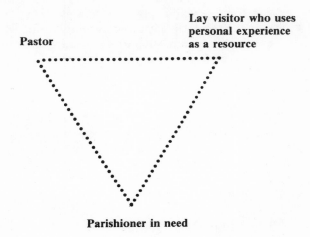

The pastor, as a professional, offers his or her training and experience as an objective observer. A lay person who has had an illness or problem and is successfully working it out can help others through his or her own suffering. This firsthand experience often offers an empathetic identity with a person that can facilitate rapid healing. The two helpers supplement one another.

Examples of this helping strategy would be the pastor and widows and/or widowers ministering to those newly bereaved. Also, a pastor trained to work with alcoholics could be a group leader with a recovered alcoholic. This triangle approach uses the best of two types of knowledge, and each compensates for weaknesses in the other. One is experiential knowledge (firsthand experience); the other is the more objective scientific knowledge and experience from many contacts with the same problem.

Jesus received reports from the ministry of the apostles (Luke 10:17). So will the pastor receive reports from his helpers. He will use them to monitor the motivation, moods, and needs of the visitors. If they are discouraged or overworked, he will note this. These reports will also give him insight into the needs of the congregation.

The Approval of the Church's Administrative Board—This approval is necessary to protect the visitors should they make

MY PERSONAL COMMITMENT

I believe God has called me to the work of lay shepherding. I will accept visitation assignments. I will attend the regularly scheduled meetings of the visitation group for fellowship, support, and continuing education for one year from this date.

NAME _____

ADDRESS _____

HOME PHONE _____ BUSINESS PHONE _____
                        (If you wish to be called)

Date _____

I wish to do the following kinds of visitation:
(Check as many as you wish)

1. Hospital
2. Nursing Home
3. Shut-ins
4. Bereavement
5. Special needs (prison, family problems, etc.)
6. Apathetic (inactive members of church)
7. Evangelistic

mistakes or meet opposition. The church board's endorsement makes lay visitation an official program of the church with its own priority among other ministries.

A budget will be necessary. Expenses include training aids and books, honorariums for consultants, training retreat expenses, and administrative/office expenses.

A Core of Committed, Mature Lay Visitors—Commitment is essential to all visitors, but there should be an inner group on fire to whom others come for warmth. Visitation is a difficult ministry and at times very anxiety producing. There will be dry times when, like the Hebrews who wished to return to Egypt, the visitors will want to leave the program. Commitments are for one year. Renewals may be made. These renewal times can also be used for training retreats which deepen knowledge and train new visitors.

Fortunate is the group with several persons possessing natural abilities in problem solving and shepherding: persons of "good repute, full of the Spirit and of wisdom" (Acts 6:3). Dr. Samuel Southard's list of natural abilities includes warmth, honesty, and insight.[4] Jesus had compassion (warmth), and he healed. Honesty begins with honest self-appraisal of one's strengths and limitations. Insight includes insight into one's own self as well as knowledge of the situation of the other person in need.

Maturity includes access to professional training and experience in counseling if such is not present in the lay shepherd. The necessary maturity would include these professions: (1) medicine, especially psychiatry, clinical psychology, nursing and paramedical training; (2) guidance counseling; (3) social and rehabilitation work. Maturity can also be found in those who have devoted years of volunteer work in institutions.

A Church Membership Large Enough to Furnish Leadership and an Outreach with Sufficient Need to Keep the Visitors Active— One church which received lay shepherding training had over 1,200 members. But the congregation was healthy and mostly consisted of young adults. Two persons a week in the hospital was a "sick week"! And only one member was a nursing home resident! In a situation such as this, it is essential that the church reach beyond its own membership. Indeed, a first question to be asked and answered is, "Will we minister to membership only, or shall we reach out into the community?"

Needs are not hard to find. Nursing home residents are frequently lonely and desire more recreational opportunities and worship and religious study experiences. Many religious groups assume pastoral responsibility for out-of-town hospitalized members of their religion. One pastor announced that a church member who had had a heart attack while on a trip had been "adopted" by the First United Methodist Church of that city.

A Carefully Written "Contract"—The contract should include:

a) Selection by the visitor of the type visits desired. A sample commitment form is included on page 94.

b) Willingness to be nurtured and guided or disciplined (or in more traditional terms, "mutual edification" and "fraternal correction") in the monthly reporting, sustaining, and training sessions. The visitor must also be willing to do the same for the other visitors. The truth may make you furious before it makes you free. But the truth (lovingly given) in the feedback of visitation efforts is essential. We learn from our mistakes; we note and strengthen our successful efforts. Both kinds of information are necessary for growth.

c) A commitment to attend follow-up sessions and to engage in reading and training experiences. The appendix contains group-learning activities and books profitable for further study. We will continue to give only as we continue to be fed. Visitation is an open system. If it becomes closed, the visitor will fall away as a leaf in the autumn.

A Lay Coordinator of "Good Repute, Full of the Spirit and of Wisdom" (Acts 6:3)—A lay coordinator is the pastor's backup when he or she is on vacation or ill or cannot be contacted. Also, pastors move on, and the lay coordinator can provide continuity in leadership. He or she may also know the visitors and those to be visited as well or better than the pastor and with the pastor can match the person in need with the best visitor. Dr. Southard suggests four additional duties:

1. Coordinate program efforts such as arranging schedules for meetings and supervising the flow of information. . . .
2. Maintain records and provide periodic reports to leaders and pastor. . . .
3. Assist new lay visitors.
4. Maintain the schedule of speakers and consultants for training programs.[5]

The actual assignment of lay coordinator duties would be a matter of business for every church to decide. Those duties would depend on the time available, leadership style, and the importance of this ministry to the pastor; they would also depend on the time, experience, skills, and commitment of the lay coordinator, and the volume of work. Other factors could be listed. But the final determination on these matters will be unique to each church.

A SUGGESTED FORMAT FOR MONTHLY FOLLOW-UP MEETINGS

1. Continuing education theory, reading reports, etc.
2. Reports and discussion of actual visits and/or proposed visits
3. Visitation assignments
4. Intercessory prayers by lay shepherds
5. Pastoral prayer

The group involvement study materials which follow by chapter numbers are designed to be used by an ongoing lay support and service group. Also, groups may read and discuss the books and articles found under the heading "Additional Study."

Chapter 1: The Authority and Context for the Lay Shepherding Ministry

Lecture or report highlights of this chapter. (This technique can be used for each chapter if appropriate.)

DISCUSSION QUESTIONS

1. Considering the changes in the form of health care from the New Testament period to today, and especially the government's involvement, how important is a visitation healing ministry at the local church level?
2. What priority would you place on the ministry of mutual edification and fraternal correction in your local church when compared with evangelism, mission, education, Christian social concerns, etc.?
3. What role in lay shepherding should be assigned to the pastor that will be faithful to the Christian tradition of lay shepherding?
4. Using McNeill's *A History of the Cure of Souls* and other sources, have someone make a report on "The History of Lay Shepherding" in your denomination.

ADDITIONAL STUDY—Read *Comprehensive Pastoral Care* by Samuel Southard (Judson Press, 1975).

Chapter 2: The Christian's Ministry to Those in Crisis

1. Invite a professional counselor to present a program showing the characteristics seen in persons with a high suicide potential and/or to describe the treatment facilities in the community (suicide prevention center, Help-Line telephone service, etc.); include a discussion on ways the agency and church can cooperate.
2. Have someone present a true case of crisis and list the resources available to that person.

DISCUSSION QUESTIONS

1. Answer the question I asked my six friends: When your life has been its roughest and you were severely tested or tempted, how did you handle it? Compare the group's answers with the summary given in this chapter.
2. The listening ministry is important, but what can be done by your group to help persons in crisis maintain their homelife with a minor degree of disruption?

ROLE PLAY*—Mr. Smyth is a forty-nine-year-old executive vice-president. He is a "Sunday-morning-Christian" but does give generously to the budget. He has been in the hospital for six weeks with a heart condition, but he is going home tomorrow. Mr. Smyth has become a "cardiac invalid," afraid to do anything. He says to you, "I don't think I should go home. I'm not strong enough. It frightens me to think I won't be able to get back to the hospital in time if I should have another attack." Respond to Mr. Smyth's need.

ADDITIONAL STUDY—Lay persons who are already in professional helping roles (social workers, guidance counselors, etc.) will be helped to minister from a Christian perspective by reading *Crisis Counseling* by Howard W. Stone (Fortress Press, 1976).

Chapter 3: Ministering to Those Who Grieve

DISCUSSION QUESTIONS

1. In your fondest dreams and hopes, what do you envision life after death to be?

*To the leader: Feel free to complete the personality of all role-play characters and situations. You may wish to create actual situations. If so, please do not betray confidences or embarrass anyone who might be known to the group members.

2. In your lowest despondency, what do you dread the most about life after death?
3. In discussing the idea of "help that is helpful," think back to a time after a loved one died.
   a. What did people say or do that was helpful to you in working through your grief?
   b. What did people say or do that was harmful?
   c. Reflecting upon that time, what do you wish people had done or said to help you?

ROLE PLAY—Mrs. Akins is a recent thirty-six-year-old widow and a member of your Sunday school class. She has called you on the phone and hysterically says, "I set the table for Jim tonight. After a month, I set the table. How could I do that? I went to pieces and so did the children!"

ADDITIONAL STUDY—Read *When Someone Dies* by Edgar Jackson (Fortress Press, 1971).

Chapter 4: The ABC's of Institutional Visitation

For this session, invite someone from a local hospital to: (1) explain the hospital's policy toward visitors; and (2) describe for you a "typical" first day, "typical" surgical day, "typical" postsurgical day, etc., from the staff's point of view.

DISCUSSION QUESTIONS
1. Think back to a time when you or an intimate family member was hospitalized. What was said or done by friends and church members that was helpful? Harmful? Also, what were the circumstances that made visits helpful or harmful?
2. Justify your visitation by listing characteristics which make your visit more helpful than a social call by a church member.

ROLE PLAY
1. Have someone play the role of "patient." Another person (or two) will be "visitors." Set up an actual or a "typical" situation. As a starter, consider the following: The patient was admitted yesterday for surgery tomorrow at 7:30 A.M. He has just come from X ray and is eating a late lunch (2:15 P.M.). The visitors do not know the nature of the surgery. The patient is not known personally by the visitors but has been seen by them at church services. The patient likewise knows his visitors only by sight as

fellow church members.

2. Design several probable situations (a woman following major female surgery, a man just out of the intensive care unit, a person in for a physical to determine the source of internal pain, etc.). Add the other necessary details such as the age of the patient, the activity in church life (a "pillar," occasional attender of worship, etc.). Role-play ways in which you would introduce the purpose of your visit.

Chapter 5: Hope and Healing

Ask a professional counselor to make a report containing the following:

1. What are the physical emotions and spiritual symptoms of depression and hopelessness?
2. What techniques are suggested for helping the depressed, hopeless-feeling patient?

The leader will close the session with a summary of the contributions made by the members of the class and a summary of topics which have been discussed in depth.

DISCUSSION QUESTIONS

1. Which of the hope-producing suggestions and ideas have you personally experienced?
2. Ask the class members to describe three or four critical incidents they have had with persons expressing hopelessness and how they responded to them. A critical incident is an actual experience and its consequences. Be precise in presenting emotions and behavior.

ROLE PLAY OF CRITICAL INCIDENTS

1. Either create a "typical incident" or role-play the incidents described in discussion #2, above.
2. Don is a fifty-five-year-old used-car salesman. He has been a member of your Sunday school class for one year and is in the second week of rehabilitation for a stroke. He can talk but is paralyzed on the left side. His recovery is not "fast enough," and he is impatient and depressed. He is a "talker," and his anxiety has aggravated this character trait. It is hard to break in and respond to him. Two children have finished college; one is a high school senior. His wife teaches in the high school. In this role play two people visit him; one of them is the class teacher.

Chapter 6: Listening That Develops Wholeness

DISCUSSION QUESTIONS

1. Ask the lay shepherds to list their personal listening techniques that need strengthening and those now strong which can be built upon.
2. Ask the students to assemble into buzz groups of four or five. One or two should present a critical incident in which someone was in great emotional turmoil. What was said or done by comforters that helped and/or hindered the problem?
3. The chapter lists, without comment, five barriers. Select one or two and ask the students to discuss how they overcame them and thereby made listening more creative for someone.

ROLE PLAY

1. Ms. Joyce Smith, a divorcee, is employed as a secretary. She has three children at home and is a member of your Sunday school class. You have known each other and her ex-husband for ten years. She is in the hospital for tests. The problem is headaches. You know, though, that her sixteen-year-old son was arrested last month for shoplifting and has been sent home for loitering after midnight in the loading zone of a warehouse. After several minutes of social talk, she says to you, "Teenagers today are more than parents can handle." In a role-play situation have two lay shepherds take it from the "teenagers today . . ." opening given by Ms. Smith.
2. Mrs. Johnson is a highly emotional person. She is in the hospital for a hysterectomy tomorrow and is in a highly anxious state. Calm her feelings.
3. Mr. Overstreet, a fifty-five-year-old Sunday school teacher, is "Mr. Calm-and-Collected." He is going to surgery tomorrow and is uptight. You observe his body language communicating tenseness. His words of faith sound hollow and unconvincing: "I know God is with me, and everything will be A-OK." Respond to *him*.

ADDITIONAL STUDY

1. *The Art of Counseling* by Rollo May is an old book but is very good and is in paperback. It was originally printed in 1939 by Abingdon Press.
2. *The Minister's Wife as Counselor* by Wallace Denton, though written for wives of clergy, has many helpful suggestions on

counseling that can be used by all lay persons (The Westminster Press, 1966).

Chapter 7: Praying with the Sick

DISCUSSION QUESTIONS
1. Compose a prayer you would use with the Mr. Jones in the
   chapter. Share it with the group.
2. How do you respond to the idea that the main purpose of healing prayer is "relating the person to the presence of God"?

ROLE PLAY—Mr. James has been a practicing Christian, but after
his son's death last year he became bitter and quit church. You are
visiting him in the hospital. All has gone well in the visit. As you
prepare to leave, you ask if he would like to have prayer. He says,
"No, I prayed for my son's life, and God didn't answer it. I don't think
one now will help either." Respond to Mr. James.

ADDITIONAL STUDY
1. Read the prayers in the Psalms. Make yourself a list that could
   be used for:
   a. People in crisis,
   b. People needing support in time of illness, bereavement,
      financial failure, etc.
2. Read *Understanding Prayer* by Edgar Jackson (World
   Publishing Co., Inc., 1968).

Chapter 8: Personal Lay Pastoral Evangelism

DISCUSSION QUESTIONS—Fear of doing harm to a patient plus
the desire that no one be lost can immobilize a lay visitor. Discuss the
appropriateness of the following suggestions for initiating a
discussion of the quality of relationship a person has with God.
1. Get to know the person through friendly conversation while
   looking for an "opening."
2. Give a brief witness of the benefits Christ has made in your life.
3. Ask the question "While you have been sick, have you been
   thinking much about your life?"
4. Offer the patient your prayers and the prayers of your religious
   support group (prayer group, Sunday school class, etc.). The
   offer should be made in such a manner that there are no strings
   attached, that is, no demands made on the person.

ROLE PLAY—Have some members present an actual visitation situation. Create the life situation of the patient and role-play how an evangelistic portion of the visit might go.

ADDITIONAL STUDY—Read *Pastoral Evangelism* by Samuel Southard (Broadman Press, 1962).

Chapter 9: The Church's Supportive Ministry

DISCUSSION QUESTIONS

1. Have the group discuss a personal experience with a person exhibiting the "giving-up—given-up" complex. Now plan a counseling program that you think would be helpful.
2. Divide into subgroups of four or five and discuss ways you were or were not supported at some time in your life. Concentrate upon resources that were available to you at that time. Were they used?

ROLE PLAY

1. James Jackson, a sixty-five-year-old widower, is in the hospital. He has had colon surgery, and the tumor is malignant. He knows his condition and does not want to live with a colostomy. He has two married children and five "grands," two being preschoolers who live a few blocks from him. Mr. Jackson has been an active person, and he retired two months before his surgery. His will to live is low. Help him face (support him in) this crisis of retirement and illness.
2. Role-play an actual situation brought by someone in the group in which support in an unchanging situation is needed.

ADDITIONAL STUDY—Read chapter 8, "Types of Supportive Counseling," in *Basic Types of Pastoral Counseling* by Howard Clinebell, Jr. (Abingdon Press, 1966).

Chapter 10: The Care and Feeding of Lay Shepherding Groups

DISCUSSION QUESTIONS

1. How would you design a lay visitation program in your church without the pastor's leadership? Or would you?
2. Which of the organization forms listed on the first page of this chapter would best serve your church?

Notes

Chapter 1   The Authority and Context for the Lay Shepherding Ministry

[1] *The Relation of Christian Faith to Health,* adopted by the 172nd General Assembly, May, 1960, The United Presbyterian Church in the United States of America, Paul Warren, Chairman, p. 14. Issued by the Office of the General Assembly, Witherspoon Building, Philadelphia, Pennsylvania.

[2] *Ibid.,* p. 15.

[3] R. K. Harrison, "Healing," *The Interpreter's Dictionary of the Bible* (Nashville: Abingdon Press, 1962), vol. 2, p. 541. This is also Paul Tournier's conclusion. See chapter 28, "The Highest Good," *A Doctor's Casebook in the Light of the Bible* (New York: Harper & Row, Publishers, Inc., 1954), p. 30.

[4] Tournier, *op. cit.,* p. 27.

[5] *The Relation of Christian Faith to Health,* p. 26.

[6] Tournier, *op. cit.,* p. 210.

[7] R. K. Harrison, *The Interpreter's Dictionary of the Bible* (Nashville: Abingdon Press, 1962), vol. 2, p. 547.

[8] Don S. Browning, *The Moral Context of Pastoral Care* (Philadelphia: The Westminster Press, 1976), p. 98.

[9] *Ibid.,* p. 114.

[10] *Ibid.,* p. 122.

[11] *Ibid.,* pp. 129-130.

[12] *Ibid.,* p. 91.

[13] Victor R. Fuchs, *Who Shall Live?* (New York: Basic Books, Inc., Publishers, 1975), p. 55. Dr. Fuchs is quoting from René Dubos, *The Mirage of Health* (New York: Harper & Row, Publishers, Inc., 1959), p. 110.

[14] John T. McNeill, *A History of the Cure of Souls* (New York: Harper & Row, Publishers, Inc., 1951), p. 311.

[15] John Wesley, *Journal,* ed. Nehemiah Curnock (London: The Epworth Press, 1938), vol. 1, pp. 197-205.

Chapter 2 The Christian's Ministry to Those in Crisis

[1] Gerald Caplan, *Principles of Preventive Psychiatry* (New York: Basic Books, Inc., Publishers, 1964). See the second chapter of this book.
[2] *Ibid.*, p. 48.
[3] *Ibid.*, p. 46.
[4] *Ibid.*, p. 48.
[5] *Ibid.*, p. 45.
[6] Howard J. Clinebell, Jr., *Basic Types of Pastoral Counseling* (Nashville: Abingdon Press, 1966), p. 164.
[7] Caplan, *op. cit.*, p. 43.
[8] Rudolph Grantham, *The Healing Relationship* (Nashville: The Upper Room, 1972), p. 11.

Chapter 3 Ministering to Those Who Grieve

[1] Edgar Jackson, *Telling a Child About Death* (New York: Channel Press, 1965; reprint ed., New York: Hawthorn Books, Inc., 1973), pp. 58-59.
[2] E. Lindemann, "Symptomatology and Management of Acute Grief," *American Journal of Psychiatry,* vol. 101 (1944), pp. 141-148.
[3] Bernard Schoenberg, et al., eds., *Loss and Grief: Psychological Management in Medical Practice* (New York: Columbia University Press, 1970), pp. 30-31.
[4] *Ibid.*, pp. 36-37.
[5] *Ibid.*, p. 31.
[6] Howard J. Clinebell, Jr., *Basic Types of Pastoral Counseling* (Nashville: Abingdon Press, 1966), p. 169.

Chapter 4 The ABC's of Institutional Visitation: Hospital and Nursing Home

[1] John L. Florell, "Crisis Intervention in Orthopedic Surgery," *Special Bulletin on Pastoral Care* (Chicago: The American Protestant Hospital Association, March, 1973), pp. 29-36.

Chapter 5 Hope and Healing

[1] Paul W. Pruyser, "On Phenomenology and Dynamics of Hoping," *Journal of the Scientific Study of Religion,* vol. 3 (October, 1963), p. 94.
[2] Lawrence L. LeShan, "Mobilizing the Life Force: An Approach to the Problem of Arousing the Sick Patient's Will to Live," *Pastoral Psychology,* vol. 17 (October, 1966), pp. 25-26.
[3] Pruyser, *op. cit.*, p. 95.
[4] LeShan, *op. cit.*, p. 22.
[5] Pruyser, *op. cit.*, p. 91.
[6] *Ibid.*
[7] Arthur J. Deikman, "Bimodal Consciousness," *Archives of General Psychiatry,* vol. 25 (December, 1971), pp. 481-489.
[8] Pruyser, *op. cit.*, p. 92.
[9] LeShan, *op. cit.*, p. 22.

Chapter 6 Listening That Develops Wholeness

[1] William B. Oglesby, Jr., "Pastoral Care and Counseling in Biblical Perspective," *Interpretation,* vol. 27, no. 3 (1973), pp. 325ff.

Chapter 7　Praying with the Sick

[1] Lewis Maclachlan, *How to Pray for Healing* (London: James Clarke & Co., 1955), pp. 91-92.

[2] Leslie D. Weatherhead, *A Shepherd Remembers* (London: Hodder and Stoughton Ltd., 1937), pp. 171-172.

Chapter 8　Personal Lay Pastoral Evangelism

[1] Karl Menninger, *The Vital Balance: The Life Process in Mental Health and Illness* (New York: The Viking Press, 1963), pp. 357-400.

[2] Gerald Caplan, *Principles of Preventive Psychiatry* (New York: Basic Books, Inc., Publishers, 1964), pp. 53-54.

[3] Samuel Southard, *Pastoral Evangelism* (Nashville: Broadman Press, 1962), p. 18.

[4] *Ibid.*, p. 24.

Chapter 9　The Church's Supportive Ministry

[1] Howard J. Clinebell, Jr., *Basic Types of Pastoral Counseling* (Nashville: Abingdon Press, 1966), pp. 139-140.

[2] *Ibid.*, p. 236. See also pp. 144-146, where Clinebell discusses the factors in low ego strength.

[3] John B. Cobb, Jr., *Theology and Pastoral Care* (Philadelphia: Fortress Press, 1977), p. 21.

[4] George L. Engel, "A Life Setting Conducive to Illness: The Giving-Up–Given-Up Complex," *Bulletin of the Menninger Clinic,* vol. 32, no. 6 (November, 1968), p. 360. Reproduced in *Psychodynamics of Patient Care* by Lawrence H. Schwartz and Jane Linker Schwartz (Englewood Cliffs, N.J.: Prentice Hall, 1972), pp. 270-272.

[5] Paul Tournier, *A Doctor's Casebook in the Light of the Bible* (New York: Harper & Row, Publishers, Inc., 1954), p. 220.

Chapter 10　The Care and Feeding of Lay Shepherding Groups: A Closing Word to Pastors and Lay Shepherds

[1] Charles A. Van Wagner II, "Supervision of Lay Pastoral Care," *The Journal of Pastoral Care*, vol. 31, no. 3 (September, 1977), p. 158.

[2] Wayne E. Oates, "Pastoral Supervision Today," *Pastoral Psychology,* vol. 24 (Fall, 1975), p. 27.

[3] Quoted in an article by H. Thomas Walker, "You Have Counseling Strength," *The Circuit Rider*, vol. 1 (May, 1977), p. 13.

[4] Samuel Southard, *Comprehensive Pastoral Care* (Valley Forge: Judson Press, 1975), p. 75.

[5] *Ibid.*, pp. 62-63.

Bibliography

For the Laity and the Pastor

Florell, John L., "Crisis Intervention in Orthopedic Surgery," *Special Bulletin on Pastoral Care*. Chicago: The American Protestant Hospital Association (March, 1973).

Foshee, Howard B., *The Ministry of the Deacon*. Nashville: Convention Press, 1968.

Grantham, Rudolph, *The Healing Relationship*. Nashville: The Upper Room, 1972.

Jackson, Edgar N., *Telling a Child About Death*. New York: Hawthorn Books, Inc., 1965.

_____, *Understanding Prayer*. Cleveland: World Publishing Co., Inc., 1968.

_____, *When Someone Dies*. Philadelphia: Fortress Press, 1971.

LeShan, Lawrence L., "Mobilizing the Life Force: An Approach to the Problem of Arousing the Sick Patient's Will to Live," *Pastoral Psychology* (October, 1966).

Moody, Raymond A., Jr., *Life After Life*. Harrisburg, Pa.: Stackpole Books, 1976.

Southard, Samuel, *Comprehensive Pastoral Care: Enabling the Laity to Share in Pastoral Ministry*. Valley Forge: Judson Press, 1975.

_____, *Pastoral Evangelism*. Nashville: Broadman Press, 1962.

Tournier, Paul, *A Doctor's Casebook in the Light of the Bible*. New York: Harper & Row, Publishers, Inc., 1954.

For the Pastor

Ashbrook, James B., and Walaskay, Paul W., *Christianity for Pious Skeptics*. Nashville: Abingdon Press, 1977.

Browning, Don S., *The Moral Context of Pastoral Care*. Philadelphia: The Westminster Press, 1976.

Clinebell, Howard J., Jr., *Basic Types of Pastoral Counseling*. Nashville: Abingdon Press, 1966.

McNeill, John T., *A History of the Cure of Souls*. New York: Harper & Row, Publishers, Inc., 1951.

Menninger, Karl, *The Vital Balance: The Life Process in Mental Health and Illness*. New York: The Viking Press, 1963.

Schoenberg, Bernard, et al., eds., *Loss and Grief: Psychological Management in Medical Practice*. New York: Columbia University Press, 1970.

Switzer, David K., *The Dynamics of Grief: Its Sources, Pain, and Healing*. Nashville; Abingdon Press, 1970.

Van Wagner, Charles A., II, "Supervision of Lay Pastoral Care," *The Journal of Pastoral Care,* vol. 31, no. 3 (September, 1977).